D0868182

making the
Switch
to being
Rich

A Guide for Those Who Care
About People and the Planet

By Steve Capellini

Royal T Press

Royal Treatment Enterprises   6461 SW 73rd Street, Miami, FL 33143

Visit our website at www.makingtheswitchtobeingrich.com.

Published by Royal T Press in association with Carlisle Ryan Digital Services

Printed in the United States of America

R|P A Royal Treatment Enterprises Company

10 9 8 7 6 5 4 3 2 1
Library of Congress Control Number: 2006902550
ISBN: 0-9779163-0-8
ISBN: 978-0-9779163-0-6

for Phyllis Sandler, mentor and friend
You truly inspired me to Make the Switch

Acknowledgments

I'd like to thank Ted Patrick for his profound and humbling lessons and for providing the underpinnings of this entire book. Also, thanks to my mother and father who had the courage and strength to hire Ted and free my mind from a destructive cult. I hope to be equally as strong for my own family—Atchana, Brandon, Tyler, and Umpun. Profound gratitude goes out to agent Jennifer Cayea who has kept believing in my work in spite of all the rejections. Lynda Solien-Wolfe continues to inspire me and offer an unending source of creative ideas; thank you, Lynda. And thanks to Mercedez Calleros whose faith in my abilities has allowed me to take those abilities to a new level. Monica Roseberry graciously offered me the title for the last chapter. Dave Kennedy gave me early inspiration on the concept of this book. Rebecca Razo rendered a thorough and creative editing to the manuscript and helped me shape it. My project editor Judy Ludowitz shepherded the manuscript through several stages with professionalism and great enthusiasm. I'd like to thank her and the whole team. And thanks to Carlisle Ryan Digital Services for printing a superior product.

Contents

Is This Book for You?

This is not a business book for business people. Rather, **ARE YOU** ...

- a **TEACHER** who believes deeply in your students and feels passionate about your career but hates the fact that you are underpaid?
- a **CHIROPRACTOR** who wants to make a difference but feels forced to deliver second-rate care by the realities of the business?
- a **PSYCHOTHERAPIST** who offers life-changing insights but struggles with your own sense of financial self-worth?
- a **MASSAGE THERAPIST** who wants to relieve the stress and enhance the health of every person you touch, but are stressed out yourself about your finances and future?
- a **NURSE** who literally helps save lives but hates your job and can't stand the thought of showing up for more drudgery at the impersonal mega-hospital where you work?
- a **RESTAURANT OWNER, COOK, OR SERVER** seemingly more talented at offering great service and tasty cuisine than you are in creating a profitable business?
- an **ENTREPRENEUR** trying to make a difference in the world with a great new product or venture but find yourself fixated on financial problems instead?
- a **FIREFIGHTER OR POLICE OFFICER** who wants to protect and serve but feels dissatisfied with the living you make and is seeking alternative sources of wealth?
- a **DENTIST** or **DOCTOR** who wants to treat your patients as more than just numbers but feels forced to work in a soul-less system and still not making the money you dream of?
- an **ACTIVIST** at a non-profit or volunteer organization on a crusade to save the world, but feel handcuffed by a shortage of funds to fulfill your mission?

- a **LAWYER** who started out wanting to fight wrongdoing and oppression but ended up cynical, disillusioned, and focused on a meaningless pursuit of money?

- a **SOLDIER** dedicated to protecting and defending your country but who feels you are somehow not allowed to enjoy all of the golden opportunities your country can provide?

- an **ARTIST, WRITER, OR PERFORMER** whose goal is to share truths, insight, and beauty with others but who feels you're prostituting yourself with less than meaningful work just to get by?

- an **ENVIRONMENTALIST** who crusades for the rights of endangered species but who feels endangered yourself because you can't seem to get out from under crushing debt?

- a **VISIONARY** involved in publishing, recording, production, design, promotion, or marketing, eager to get your voice heard, but working for a conglomerate hawking products of questionable value to mankind?

- a **YOGA TEACHER**, fitness instructor, health expert, or lifestyle coach who uplifts and inspires others, but you're still struggling to lift your own life up out of money concerns?

- a **PROMOTER** of causes or individuals who have something to say, an agent, manager, or publicist who finds it hard to promote your own dreams and plans?

- a **SOCIAL WORKER** who fights for the rights of the underprivileged but has trouble standing up for your own rights when it's time to talk money?

- a **STUDENT** who despairs of ever finding a true path—a path with value and meaning that will still allow you to make a good living?

- a **BANK TELLER, STORE CLERK, LABORER, OR UNEMPLOYED INDIVIDUAL** who wants desperately to do something to make your mark on the world but haven't yet been able to escape the rat race?

In short, is it a matter of pride that you care more about **WHAT YOU DO** and **WHO YOU ARE** than how much money you make? And yet money, or the lack of it, still causes much frustration in your life?

Do you feel a great yearning to live a life with **PURPOSE**, but feel partially blocked from leading that life due to a lack of funds?

Then we need to talk. . .

Introduction

Don't Read this book
if all you want
is Money

This is not a typical get-rich book and it's not for everyone. In fact, in order to be truly effective, this book makes a few assumptions about you, the reader:

1. You care about your world and the people in it.
2. The fate of the planet matters to you.
3. You hope to meld your work life with your highest aspirations.
4. You want what you do to help people.
5. You need more money to do the things you want and make a positive influence on others, but you're tied down to the money-making mechanics of everyday life.
6. It sometimes feels as if those who don't care as much about others or the planet are the ones who have more than their share of the wealth in the world.

7. You don't know why money eludes you. It's as if there exists an invisible force-field keeping it away—a force-field that seemingly starts inside of your body and emanates outward, keeping you locked inside a "moneyless bubble" from which you have no idea how to escape.

If these describe your situation and you wish to dedicate yourself to something more than accumulating wealth for its own sake, then this is a book specifically for you. In these pages I will be speaking directly to those who have dedicated their lives to helping others and who feel the need to help the planet before it is destroyed by our own misguided actions. Why? Because I have been saddened and dispirited over the years as I've read one text after another that talks about getting money for the sake of getting money.

What's the point of money in the first place? I've come to know, as I'm sure you have, that money is "neutral"—that it is an energy or force that can be used for good, bad, and everything in between. You can feed the homeless with it, support a terrorist regime, or buy sports cars. Money, according to these books, is a science and can be boiled down to mathematical equations. It can be quantified in supply and demand curves. It can be marshaled through enlightened capitalism to support the greater good. This is all true, but it is only true on one level: a superficial level.

Money is something beyond all this. While it is certainly mundane and mathematical, and based on the capacity to produce and distribute goods and services, it is at the same time something more, what some might even call "spiritual." Can you feel it? That force that seems to put money into some people's hands while keeping it out of the hands of others? Why is it that so many people who seem to care very little for others or the environment often end up with an inordinate percentage of the world's available cash? Why is it that we, the ones who do care, end up with so little? These are the questions that this book hopes to help answer for you. It is going to take you deep inside of yourself to some places you might not have searched when you looked for success in the past. It is going to examine some internal processes of your mind and personality, revealing how you may in fact be standing in your own way, blocking your own road to financial freedom.

If all you want is a Lamborghini and another vacation home, do yourself a favor and put this book down right now. If, on the other hand, you want financial freedom, and with that freedom you hope to help others and make a difference, then read on. My deepest hope is that the following story will ignite a spark in your mind that will light the way toward a new understanding of your life and how you can live it, because I believe that you—that we—deserve the prosperity that will enable us to pursue our dreams. And why not? Why shouldn't the people who care, who help, who touch others' lives, attain the resources and freedoms we need?

This book is written for you if you are "one of us." It's for you if you're a therapist, teacher, nurse, bodyworker, physician, caretaker, social worker, artist, promoter, visionary, entrepreneur, guide, counselor, peace activist, environmentalist, or volunteer worker. It's for you if you live to protect, serve and uplift others. This book is also for you if you wish you were one of these people but are not because you're too busy scrabbling away at a job you don't like in order to pay the bills.

I want to help you soar, because you deserve to soar. You are worthy. All human beings are intrinsically worthy at birth, but those who have dedicated themselves to helping others are particularly worthy. They have earned it.

I believe we can help more, do more, care more, and live bigger lives but only if we are willing to courageously explore our own minds first. My own exploration was forced upon me in a dramatic way, during a kidnapping and hostage situation in Colorado. I think this story will help you understand your own situation much better, and so I'd like to share it with you. It began in a dark Denver basement, several years ago, where a powerfully built black man in a business suit towered over me and began what would become one of the greatest lessons of my life. . .

A Dark Denver Basement

"You are a mindless robot," said the man. "Everything you think or say has been conditioned by somebody else. It's as if you're acting on remote control. I know exactly what you're thinking and can tell you exactly how you'll respond to any question because I know what the people who control your mind have been telling you. And I can prove it."

These were the words spoken to me in that dark Denver basement one December evening just before Christmas. The man speaking was Ted Patrick, the most famous "deprogrammer" in the world. Patrick specializes in de-brainwashing people who have become caught up in cults, which is precisely what had happened to me. Like many idealistic young people, fresh out of college and intent on helping others, I was dissatisfied with the status quo and actively seeking answers to life's more important questions. A group known as the Unification Church, or "Moonies," got hold of me through dubious recruiting tactics, and its leaders gradually convinced me that the world was organized a certain way. They couched their explanations in well-known historical and religious contexts so that everything made perfect sense. It went something like this: Jesus, Mohammed, Buddha, and other great spiritual leaders had come to save the world, but they failed. The truth of that was all around us in the obviously unsaved world with its miseries and inequalities abounding. Though they had failed, these leaders had still managed to set the stage for the one true leader who would be able to finish the job: the Reverend Sun Myung Moon.

Looking back, of course, I see that Moon was not the messiah he claimed to be. And I have since asked myself on many occasions, "What if Ted Patrick had not spoken those words to me in that Denver basement? What if my family hadn't paid Patrick thousands of dollars and gambled on losing me forever in a risky kidnapping? Would I still be a 'mindless robot'? Would my view of the world still be skewed to fit that of the group?"

Since that day, I have, understandably, done a lot of thinking and a good deal of research into the meaning of such terms as "brainwashing" and "mind control." And at the same time I have continued to ask myself those important questions: What's life all about? What is truly important? How can I help others? These musings eventually led me into the profession of massage therapy, hands-on healing, and a career in the health spa industry. This was the particular path that helped answer some of those questions for me. I found a way to connect to other people, to help some of them and to make a difference. It has been a good life, and it's only getting better.

Along the way I also started to notice something strange. Many people in the healing and helping professions, myself included, experience an inexplicably negative relationship with money in general and their own finances in particular. I personally know dozens of therapists, social workers, activists, and practitioners who struggle from month to month to pay the bills. I myself lived for years in this manner. It was an endless cycle: work to help people, make a little money, spend all the money on rent, bills, and sometimes a little fun, then start all over again. There seemed to be no way out.

One day it dawned on me just how ridiculous the situation was. Picture the scene: I was living in Miami in the middle of the summer, in a decrepit soon-to-be-torn-down house with no air-conditioning. Scrounging around in my sweat-soaked pockets for bills and coins, I pulled out a few dollars and began to count. Could I afford the six-inch or twelve-inch sandwich for lunch at Subway™?

That's when it struck me. I mopped away the sweat from my brow, put down my pitiful pennies, and scrambled over to the counter to grab a pen and paper. What if, I scribbled, I and all of my poor, idealistic humanitarian friends were . . . mindless robots? What if our month-to-month mentality was the result of some form of mind-control that we were being subjected to without our knowledge? It certainly seemed like we were all believers in a religion that was somehow keeping us poor.

That realization was life-changing. Now, I'm living in a different world. In fact, I'm writing these very words on my laptop in First Class as I jet off to see friends and associates, expand networks, meet new colleagues, teach others what I know, help people with their careers, and make thousands of dollars doing it. How is this possible? Is it because I'm smarter than I used to be? A better therapist? More ambitious or self-confident?

I don't think so. I believe my present-day success is a direct result of the understanding I've gained into the workings of the mind. It is a result of seeing how the mind is controlled by thought patterns we are almost always unaware of. My success is a result of unearthing these patterns, bringing them to the surface and showering them with the light of conscious awareness.

Now, looking back, I consider it a great blessing that I was indoctrinated into the Moonies, that I lived with them for six months, and that my mind was molded by them into what they wanted it to be. Strange though it may sound, I feel particularly blessed to have been deprogrammed by Ted Patrick, the most flamboyant and knowledgeable man in the field, who has written a book on the topic, *Let Our Children Go*. Without intending to, Ted Patrick became a key teacher in my life. It was through his decisive words and actions during this turbulent time that I came to understand how deeper and subtler levels of mind-control are exerted upon all of us, all the time. I will forever owe a good portion of my success in life to the lessons he taught me at that crucial juncture, as well as the lessons I learned afterward through my study of books and other resources that Patrick recommended. These are the lessons I will share with you in the following chapters.

This book will explore, step-by-step, the mechanics of mind-control and how it is achieved by one individual or group over another. It will show you what brainwashing actually is. Then, it will systematically *reveal the ways in which your own thoughts have been gradually molded and controlled over your lifetime* into that of a mindless robot as far as money matters go. I trust these words will reach a deep place that helps open you to new ideas and new, more prosperous ways of being. My ultimate hope is that this book will free you to achieve more of your goals, which in turn will help more people.

So, let's begin. In the first chapter we'll take a look at the scary possibility that, indeed . . . you are a mindless robot.

April 2006

"Freedom is slavery some poets tell us.
Enslave yourself to the right leader's truth . . .
and it will set you free."

Robert Frost

You are a Mindless Robot

At first, of course, I didn't believe him. There he was, this dapper stranger, dressed in a suit, standing over me in that basement late at night, telling me I was a mindless robot. My father sat off to one side, his head hanging low, as if he were guilty of some horrible crime. All I knew at that moment was that I hated him. And I hated Ted Patrick. I also hated Patrick's two strongmen who had helped kidnap me. Once I understood what was happening, I grabbed the closest projectile I could find in that furnished basement—a jar of peanut butter—and hurled it toward the small high window. It exploded against the wall in a splatter of broken glass and brown goo. The whole scene was so strange.

Yes, I reacted very strongly against Ted Patrick when he first told me I was a mindless robot. Just about everybody does. Patrick has confronted hundreds of people just like me, and the very first thing he tells them is that they're mindless robots. Why? To get a reaction and to challenge their minds and ways of thinking. And the first reaction of a challenged mind is self-defense. Denial. No way. Not me. I'm no mindless robot. What's he talking about?

If I were to suddenly appear before you right now, forcibly maneuver you into a small room, lock the door behind you, post two guards outside, and call you a mindless robot right to your face, how do you think you'd respond?

That's right. Denial. No way. Not me. I'm no mindless robot. What's he talking about? So be warned . . . I am going to subject you to something quite similar, starting right now. In effect, if you keep reading from this point on, you are going to experience a virtual kidnapping and deprogramming of your own. You will be forcing yourself to look at things in a new way. In order to really Make the Switch to Being Rich, it is essential that you force these new ideas upon yourself, because your natural tendency will be to reject them. You'll deny everything. And that is precisely why you are in the same old economic boat today that you've always been in.

This is the first lesson that Patrick taught me. In order to change a programmed way of thinking, you have to be forced out of it. You have to be kidnapped. Your mind needs to be held hostage.

This is how it happened to me: My father came to visit me in Colorado, the main training ground for new Moonie recruits. I was selling flowers on the streets for twelve hours a day while subsisting mostly on peanut butter and jelly sandwiches, sleeping four hours a night, and attending endless lectures and prayer meetings. Though my new Moonie friends counseled me against it, my father was able to convince me to stay with him at his hotel in Denver. He said he was there on business, but unbeknownst to me he had arranged with Ted Patrick to "extract" me from the Moonies that very night.

As we drove back to the hotel from dinner, my father stopped to pick up two "hitch-hikers" who were actually Patrick's strongmen. When we dropped the two off at a suburban house, they invited us inside. As I stepped into the house, completely unaware of what was happening, the door suddenly slammed shut behind me, the bolt shot home, and I found myself suddenly a caged animal. A prisoner. That's when I threw the peanut butter jar up toward the window.

The two strongmen made sure I knew who was boss. When I made a dash for the door, one of them stood in front of it like an Arabian sentry, thick forearms folded over a muscled chest. When I started pacing my basement cell, maniacally rushing back and forth, they kept a close watch over me. The door at the top of the stairs was thick and had several locks and bolts in place. My father stared into space, then looked down at the floor in shame and occasionally stole glances at me, hoping I wouldn't explode. But I did explode.

"How could you do this to me! I can't believe this!" I shouted. "My own father. Cutting me off from my deepest desires. You have no idea what you're doing. And you'll never change me!"

He hung his head again.

It went on like this for hours. And, looking back, I see that we could have been stuck in that stalemate for days, or months, or years. Something had to happen. Some catalyst needed to be introduced in order for the deprogramming process to actually begin. That catalyst was Ted Patrick.

He blew into the room like a hurricane. Up until that point, in my own mind I felt I was becoming a stronger and stronger Moonie as each hour passed. But Patrick knew what he was doing. Within seconds, he walked straight over to me, gripped me hard by the shoulders, and forced me to sit down on a couch. I stood up. He grabbed again, pushing down harder.

"Sit down," he said with authority, in a tone of utter command. "You are a mindless robot."

As he stood there above me, I was forced into a subservient position sitting before him. This was intentional. The force of his grasp on my shoulders was intentional, too. He needed to overpower me to get his message across. He forced me to listen to what he had to say. But (and this is a crucial "but") these tactics would have been completely worthless if he didn't have the necessary information to back them up. That's why his strongmen or my father or the average person on the street would not have been able to deprogram me. They didn't have Patrick's knowledge, his information—the information you will learn in this book.

"Listen to me," Patrick said. "I'm going to fill you in on a little secret. I know how your mind is working and what the people in that group of yours have been doing to you."

"No, you don't," I said, still defiant in spite of my submissive position on the couch. "You don't have any idea what I believe. How could you?" To me, at that moment, Patrick looked like nothing more than a bully, an ignorant nonbeliever, a heathen, a criminal, a hoodlum, a thug. How could he possibly know the first thing about my fervently held spiritual beliefs? "You'll never understand," I said, then stared off into space, trying to ignore his hulking immoveable presence just two feet in front of me.

"Is that right?" he asked. "Well then why don't you and I have a little discussion about a certain technique called love-bombing."

I froze. Love-bombing. How could Patrick know about love-bombing? It was something I had come to know a lot about over the past months of my involvement with the Moonies. They had used it with me when I first visited their farm commune in Northern California. After I moved in with them and became part of the group, I started using the technique myself on newer recruits.

Love-bombing was simple. You and one or two other members were assigned a new recruit and then ganged-up on them, showering as much attention and affection as possible on them, short of sexual contact. It was hard for most people to resist this tactic. People are starved for attention. Starved for validation. Starved, often, for love. Bombing people with love is one sure way to get them to listen to what you have to say, and this is precisely what the Moonies did. After new recruits were buttered up for days with tasty food (meals were much more elaborate and wholesome for recruits than they were for members), sing-alongs, uplifting speeches, constant camaraderie, and an endless stream of ego-boosting praise, they were quite vulnerable to the next step, which consisted of overloading them with new information regarding the nature of religion and the meaning of history. Reverend Moon and his plans were never mentioned in these early days. It was all about love, and saving the Earth, and helping mankind through acts of selflessness.

At 5 a.m. every day we would awaken to the sounds of a "brother" strumming a six-string and singing a happy song:

> "When The Red, Red, Robin
> Comes bob, bob, bobbin'
> Along, along,
> There'll be no more sobbin'
> When he starts throbbin'
> His old sweet song.
>
> Wake up, wake up you sleepy head,
> Get up, get up, get out of bed,
> Cheer up, cheer up, the sun is red,
> Live, love, laugh and be happy.
> Ha, ha, ha, ha, ha, HA, HA, HA!"

It was just plain difficult to be negative while you were with these people. And we all joined in the game by showering this same positive energy on the new people. It was a self-fulfilling circle, honey-coated and superficial. But it worked. Love-bombing was a time-tested technique, one of the several that made the Moonies' recruiting tactics roughly forty times more effective than those of the twentieth century's most successful evangelist, Billy Graham.

"OK," I said to Patrick. "So you've heard about love-bombing. Big deal. Somebody told you about it. That's all. It doesn't prove anything."

But Patrick was ready for that one. "Love-bombing is only one of the tactics they used on you, Robot." For those first few days, he always referred to me as "Robot," not by my name. "There are a whole bunch of other tactics, too, and I'm going to explain them to you now, and you're going to sit there and listen. Do you understand me, Robot?"

I didn't say a word but just sat there staring past him. This, apparently, was not going to be easy. Patrick was tough. But still, my newfound faith was firm. Nothing was going to dissuade me. If anything, this whole procedure was only serving to make me stronger in my faith, more convinced than ever that Reverend Moon was who he claimed to be. I clammed up, determined to simply sit out the tirade by this big brutish thug standing above me.

"OK, Robot, listen up. I'm going to explain a little thing called mind control."

And thus began one of the most fascinating lessons of my life, although at the moment I was trying desperately to ignore it. You too will probably try to avoid hearing this lesson. While your eyes are reading these words, your mind will try to ignore them. I understand that. All I ask is that you expose your mind to the ideas presented here. You don't have to accept them. That, in essence, is what deprogramming is: forced exposure to new ideas and concepts different than those of the group that has programmed you.

Patrick then introduced me to a book that I would later read avidly. It had the imposing title, *Thought Reform and the Psychology of Totalism: A Study of Brainwashing in China,* by Dr. Robert Jay Lifton.

What could brainwashing in China possibly have to do with me, I thought? The book chronicled the techniques used by communist captors to indoctrinate prisoners into their ways of thinking. Communist indoctrination tactics? Prisoners of war in China? Surely Patrick had to be joking.

But he was not joking. For another hour he forced the pages of the book in my face and forced his words into my ears. "Listen to this, Robot. I'm going to teach you about brainwashing techniques. Then you can tell me if any of it sounds familiar."

Lifton lists eight main elements that make up "brainwashing" as practiced by the Chinese communists. These include:

1. Milieu Control
2. Mystical Manipulation
3. The Demand for Purity
4. The Cult of Confession
5. Sacred Science

6. Loading the Language
7. Doctrine Over Person
8. The Dispensing of Existence

Milieu Control

Milieu control, Patrick told me, is the most fundamental feature of any mind-controlled group. "What these groups do," he said, "is control every form of communication—what people read, observe, and discuss, and even what they say about each other. The communists in China created an environment in which neighbors spied on each other and turned each other in to the authorities. They controlled people by closely monitoring what was published in newspapers and what was allowed in public speeches. And the Moonies do the same thing."

I must have looked skeptical because Patrick suddenly bellowed at me. "This is no joke, Robot! This is exactly what's happening to you. I know it is. You can't lie to me. Those Moonies make sure you have no easy access to television or magazines, am I right? And the papers and books you read have to be 'approved' by leadership. You spend all your time reading Moonie newsletters, inspirational poems written by other Moonies, and the so-called 'Divine Principle,' Moon's version of the Bible. Just like the communists, Moonies think they've cornered the market on the truth, and they tell you all other points of view are wrong. They make you suspicious of other sources of information. This is what they're doing to you."

I had indeed experienced exactly this type of manipulation at the hands of the Moonies. For example, once when I picked up a newspaper at a convenience store, a "brother" gently took it out of my hands and placed it back on the stand. "You don't need to read about the fallen world so much any more," he said. "We're operating on a higher plane now." As Moonies, all of the information we received was controlled and choreographed.

Mystical Manipulation

"These groups are savvy," continued Patrick. "Once they've controlled your communications, they gradually bring your thoughts under their control too by bombarding you with messages about the rightness and truth of the group. Eventually, you reach a point when these thoughts seem to arise 'mystically' from inside your own mind. This 'mystical manipulation' is the real beginning of trust or faith in the message of the group. For communists, it was trust in a new world social and political order. For the Moonies, it's faith in the teachings of reverend Moon and the slanted view of history that supports his domination."

I distinctly remembered the hours I spent swaying with groups of dozens or hundreds of others, praying and singing and mouthing the praises of Reverend Moon. There was one particular moment when I ceased to be an observer of these proceedings and instead became a participant. It happened in Boulder, Colorado, at a small meeting of fellow members who had spent the day selling flowers on the street. The group leader asked me to lead the prayer before lights-out. Within moments I found myself fervidly spouting off Moon's teachings in a way that made perfect sense to me. The teachings seemed to arise from within my own mind. In that moment, I believed. I had faith. And it felt unbelievably good.

The Demand for Purity

"Converts to mind-control groups are taught to make sharp distinctions between insiders and outsiders," said Patrick. "Everything inside the group is good and pure. Everything opposed to the group is bad and impure. The whole world is neatly divided into 'good' and 'evil.' For the communists, capitalism was evil. Private ownership was evil. Religion, that great 'opiate of the masses,' was evil. Anything and everything that could be done to oppose evil was OK'd by the communists. Even mass murder.

"To be in the group, you've got to be pure. This demand for purity employs two powerful forces—guilt and shame. Because total purity is impossible to achieve, everyone in the group feels a sense of guilt all the time. This benefits those in control, who can manipulate guilt-ridden followers much easier than proud, free-thinking individuals. And everybody secretly feels shame also because they fear that everybody else knows they're falling short of this unattainable purity. Guilt and shame keep everybody purging themselves of 'sin' and denouncing the 'impure' world outside the group. Am I right? Isn't this what's happening to you?"

Indeed, the Moonies were experts at this. Although I didn't want to admit it when Patrick confronted me with the evidence, I couldn't help but remember the many times I'd witnessed group members striving to outdo each other in the shame and guilt department. People would not eat for days, publicly exclaiming that they did not "deserve" the food and that their internal demons needed to be purged through sacrifice. All sexuality was deemed impure, and "brothers" and "sisters" went to absurd extremes to avoid sexual feelings of any kind. Many of the men took long cold showers every morning and wore painfully tight-fitting underwear. Many of the women actually lost their periods and became totally asexual. And what's more, they were proud of it. The Moonies were famous for their glossy-eyed, asexual, robotic appearance, but I had always assumed it was a ridiculous parody. Now, Patrick was forcing me to consider the possibility that it was true.

Still, I wouldn't listen. I wouldn't give in to Patrick's accusations. I remained silent while he continued his tirade.

The Cult of Confession

"These groups create a 'cult of confession' to solidify their ownership of the individual," said Patrick. "They force every member to expose their innermost feelings, especially feelings of guilt, shame, and inadequacy. The Chinese communists forced their converts to confess their 'sins' against the state in huge group meetings. And many other groups have used this technique to establish firm bonds among members. Even Alcoholics Anonymous, for example, is famous for its gatherings where members publicly confess their inadequacies in order to gain group support. Did you know that? The Moonies do the exact same thing."

It was true. We would sit in groups of two-hundred or more people at a large house in Berkeley, California, and listen as one member after another, from the highest to the lowest in terms of seniority, would get up and confess how sinful they were and how incomplete their surrender was to the teachings of Reverend Moon.

Sacred Science

"Every one of these groups is the same," said Patrick. "They allow absolutely no questioning of their belief system. The person who created the group's 'sacred science' is believed to be on a higher plane, somehow exempt from logic, historical fact, or scientific evidence. It's ironic, because these leaders also claim to possess the one true logically, historically, and scientifically accurate view of the world. In the case of the communists, nobody could question the leader's actions, even when those actions caused the extermination of millions of people. You're in the same situation now with Moon. It's dangerous. Think about it."

I clearly remembered how I scoffed at Moon's teachings the first time I heard them. After months of love-bombing and other techniques, however, my scorn turned into acceptance, and I found myself believing things that on the surface seemed ridiculous. I even believed Moon's claim that children born to couples he had married in one of his mass wedding ceremonies were "without sin" and constituted a new godly race of humans. We were not allowed to question these "facts." They were beyond the need for proof.

Loading the Language

"Do you know what a 'thought-terminating cliché' is?" asked Patrick. "Dr. Lifton talks about them in his book. The communists, the Moonies, and every other mind-control group use them. They're simple words and phrases that sum up complex situations. When you use them, you not only constrict your speech, but your thoughts too. You end up with a constricted view of things in general. Your ability to explain yourself becomes stunted, and your ability to experience the world in all its fullness and shades of gray is reduced. When your language changes, your world gets changed, too. At first, a verbally narrowed point of view feels great because the world is suddenly explainable and understandable. Over time, though, your mind can't think outside this box anymore. Your imagination withers and dies. That's what's happening to you."

The Moonies loaded their language extensively. Almost every phrase that left our mouths was a cliché created by the group to easily explain away the complexities of life. For example, we called Reverend Moon "Heavenly Father," which equated him with God in our minds. Nothing he said or did could be wrong. We called our recruiting tactics "love-bombing." We called people outside the group "fallen" because they were descended from Adam and Eve who had fallen from grace through sin. I considered Ted Patrick a fallen person, and I knew he was trying to get me to admit that Reverend Moon was not who he claimed to be. So, I decided to use another Moonie technique to trick him.

"I see your point," I said. "It's very compelling. I know exactly what you're saying, and I believe you." By lying this way, I believed I would get Patrick to cease his useless attacks and let me rest.

Patrick grinned. "That's not going to work, Robot," he said.

"What do you mean?"

"You can't use 'heavenly deception' on me. I know what you're doing."

He'd caught me. In the Moonies, we were taught that it was OK to say or do anything to a fallen person, as long as it was in order to further the purposes of the group. When you were lying to an outsider, you weren't really lying—you were employing "heavenly deception." Apparently, Patrick knew all about this cliché as well.

Doctrine Over Person

"See what I'm saying?" asked Patrick. "You use this 'heavenly deception' trick because they told you to. You can't do anything but what they tell you to do. There's no room in the Moonies for renegades or rugged individuals. Everyone's personal identity has to be remolded to fit neatly inside the group. People don't matter, only doctrine. The Chinese communist party leaders didn't care if you were a great musician. They forced great musicians to work on the communal farms like everyone else. You were supposed to avoid 'sinful' self-expression. That's how people are suppressed, and that's what's happening to you. That's why you're here in Colorado selling flowers on the streets in December. You have no say in the matter. No choice. They're probably telling you it's your 'destiny' to be here, right? And you're not supposed to complain about it, either. If you did, you'd be questioning their doctrine and their sacred science. Face it: You're under their control."

The Dispensing of Existence

"I'm not under anyone's control," I said. "I make up my own mind what to say and what to do. I'm here in Denver because I want to be."

"No, you're not!" shouted Patrick. "You're here because you're terrified to death of what might happen if you don't do what they tell you to do. You believe that only by following their commands can you earn the right to exist. People outside the group, in fact, do not have the same right to exist as you members do. They are 'fallen.' They are 'impure.' They are not 'chosen.' When the day of reckoning comes, they deserve to be 'left behind.' Every single mind-control group does the same thing. They tell you you're saved and you have the right to exist, but then they fill you with fear. They tell you if you disobey or leave the group, you'll give up that right to exist. Communists who slipped outside of the party could be persecuted, imprisoned, tortured or even killed. The Moonies tell you something similar, don't they?"

We were told that if we left the group, either through our own free will or through kidnapping and deprogramming, we were giving up our place in the "heavenly kingdom" that Reverend Moon was creating. Our souls would rot away in the fallen world. Our children would turn out to be the impure sinful spawn of Satan. Our existence would cease to have any meaning.

Ted Patrick knew this. He knew I couldn't just turn and walk away from a group that held my very right to exist in its grasp. He knew I wouldn't change my mind so quickly.

"So how do you feel, Robot?" he asked. "Does any of this make sense to you?"

As Patrick knew I would, I immediately shoved all of these new ideas out of my mind. I felt strong. I felt faithful. All this scientific mumbo-jumbo about brainwashing and Chinese communists was not going to make me lose my faith. It was strange, but when he finished talking, I felt a physical sensation in my mind, almost as if my brain were restructuring itself, putting the pieces of itself back into Moonie mode. I didn't know it at the time, but I was soon going to learn how this structuring and de-structuring of the brain actually works.

For now, though, after my first session with Patrick, I was still "saved." My faith was intact. I was still a Moonie.

"That's right, Robot," he said. "Go ahead and smirk. This is just the beginning."

Finally, he turned and walked away, leaving me to sit there alone on the couch for a long time.

Chapter Two

> *"Wealth is not without its advantages, and the case to the contrary, although it has often been made, has never proved widely persuasive."*
> John Kenneth Galbraith

Money Myths of the Mindless Robots

A s far as money goes, you too are a mindless robot. You are living inside a "moneyless bubble," and millions of others just like you are in this bubble, too. You are under the control of family, culture, and society—strong influences that have taken you and molded you into a particular kind of person without your knowledge. Certain very specific indoctrination techniques have been used to achieve this. These techniques are remarkably similar to those used by the communist party in China, the Moonies, and countless other mind-control groups around the world.

I know it isn't easy to hear this, but it's the first step in breaking free from the patterns that have controlled you your entire life. I can't grasp you by the shoulders, push you down onto a couch, and force you to listen like Ted Patrick did to me. The best I can do is put these words on the page in front of you. Look at them closely and consider the possibility that

1. Regarding money and finances, you are a mindless robot.
2. Other people, and certain familial, societal, and cultural forces, have determined your attitude toward money.
3. These people and societal forces have programmed your attitudes without your knowing it.
4. In order to break free of these programmed attitudes, you first need to become aware of them.
5. Once you are aware, it is possible to break free. You must then follow certain steps to do so. You must, in effect, "deprogram" yourself from poverty consciousness. The steps in this book can help you understand how to do this.
6. You have the power within you to lead a much more fulfilling, exciting life, free from the money worries you've been programmed into experiencing in the past.

Over your lifetime, you have gradually come to believe certain powerful MONEY MYTHS that now rule your every thought and action. You have come to associate yourself very strongly with a particular group of people who share a belief in those myths. And although this group does not have an official church or meeting hall, its members nonetheless identify very strongly with each other and with their common underlying belief structure.

In this chapter, I am going to take Lifton's eight categories of thought control and show you how they apply to your situation as a member of the group who cares more about mankind, the environment, art, ideas, and spiritual matters than it does about money. As you will see, each category corresponds to a Money Myth that you, as a member of this group, have unconsciously adapted.

#	MONEY MYTH	THOUGHT CONTROL TECHNIQUE
1	MONEY IS THE ROOT OF ALL EVIL.	MILIEU CONTROL
2	YOU HAVE NOT CHOSEN YOUR ECONOMIC SITUATION.	MYSTICAL MANIPULATION
3	BY OPPOSING WEALTH, YOU BECOME PURE.	THE DEMAND FOR PURITY
4	LIKING THE THINGS MONEY CAN BUY IS A WEAKNESS.	THE CULT OF CONFESSION
5	POVERTY IS HOLY.	SACRED SCIENCE
6	YOU COULD HAVE MORE MONEY IF YOU ONLY WANTED IT, BUT YOU DON'T.	LOADING THE LANGUAGE
7	MONEY WOULD CHANGE YOU.	DOCTRINE OVER PERSON
8	IF YOU BECAME RICH, YOU WOULD CEASE TO EXIST.	THE DISPENSING OF EXISTENCE

Money Myth #1: Money Is the Root of All Evil

The very air that you breathe and the ground upon which you walk is completely saturated with your firm belief that money is the root of all evil. It is your own self-imposed form of MILIEU CONTROL, and it pervades your entire life. You confine your reading and your TV watching to those outlets that confirm your belief. You find yourself thinking (or saying out loud to like-minded individuals), "I can't believe how those greedy bastards who run things are raping and pillaging the Earth and exploiting its people, all in the pursuit of money." Or, alternatively, perhaps you find yourself watching a TV show that features wealthy people. Inevitably, their lives will be roiling cauldrons of unhappiness, despair, pointlessness, and petty competition. At best, they're bumbling idiots.

It is of course true that certain wealthy people actually are greedy, selfish, and unhappy, and that some of them exploit others for their own ends. But you, as someone who has fallen prey to Money Myth #1, believe that all people with money are greedy in this way. You believe that the root of all evil is money and that the very foundation of our economic system leads people to behave in evil ways; therefore, you naturally choose to "opt out" of the system, making just enough money to get by and afford a color TV to watch the really rich implode on the screen, but not so much that any of your peers (the other members of your moneyless group), can point to you and say, "Ah ha! You are one of the evil doers."

This belief in the evil of money is tied in with another widely held belief of the moneyless multitudes, the belief that "If you are good, good things will happen to you." I call this "the lie of karma." It has been conclusively proven beyond a shadow of a doubt that, indeed, bad things can and do happen to good people. If you think about it for a moment, you will agree. Earthquakes, floods, tsunamis, hurricanes, and the ravages of war do not just afflict the bad guys. They happen to everyone. Have children who've perished in disasters really done something bad in a previous life to deserve it? No. Yet you persist in believing it is through your striving to be "good" that you avoid bad consequences. So, you watch the right shows, buy the right eco-friendly car, think the right thoughts.

You are keeping yourself at your own economic level through your beliefs. And at the same time you communicate your beliefs to others, to let them know you're in the same group, even though you may not be aware of it. There are no secret handshakes for members to share, but you definitely have ways of identifying each other. It's in the car you drive, the clothes you wear, the style of your hair, the music you listen to, the books you read, the heroes you idolize, and those you don't. It's in the way you hold yourself and the way you walk. It's embedded in the lines and contours of your face, and it is sealed deep inside your eyeballs like a miniscule point of light encased in amber.

As a good therapist or self-sacrificing nurse or struggling physician or poor artist or angry environmentalist or dutiful teacher and as a good person in general, you have bought into this way of thinking. You think in terms of evil bosses, evil landlords, evil owners, and evil corporate CEOs who have all the money. This is where you live, it's the sea in which you swim, and it's the soup of your subconscious reality. Paradoxically, you look "down" on people who are "above" you on the economic ladder because, by definition, they must have more commerce with evil. In your world, the rich are the "outsiders"—the "fallen" who must be avoided.

Make no mistake about it—you are a victim of MILIEU CONTROL just as much as any Moonie or communist convert ever was.

Money Myth #2: You Have Not Chosen Your Economic Situation

Somehow, it seems, as if by magic or some MYSTICAL MANIPU-LATION, you simply ended up in your present economic situation. You didn't choose it; it just *happened.* And now you're stuck. But at the same time, you harbor a deep belief in the rightness of your stuck situation. It feels honorable—almost admirable. You believe that money is the root of all evil and therefore begin to have "faith" in the goodness of being in the moneyless class. It seems that you must have been born this way and it's all for the best in the end, because you'd rather not deal with all the evil that money would bring with it.

Admittedly, fate plays a part in the roll of the economic dice, and many people are faced with almost insurmountable circumstances. These are the people stuck in the slums of poor nations, with very few available resources at their disposal. If you are reading this book, however, you are probably not stuck in absolute poverty. You have many choices and potential resources available. Still, you feel stuck, unable to take advantage of those resources. You believe your economic situation has been somehow forced upon or allotted to you, and that you have no power to choose. That's a myth. The truth is that you are choosing your economic situation minute by minute with your thoughts and your actions, all of which closely mirror your self-image. This self-image has been created by your beliefs, which are generated by the milieu in which you find yourself.

Believe me, I know what it feels like to be stuck. I know how it is to dig through sweaty pockets looking for coins to buy lunch. I also know that it feels as if some outside force has created your economic situation, that you have nothing to do with it, that it's simply the job market or economy or other people's lack of understanding.

From a place deep inside, unknown to your conscious mind, you are choosing not to be on the "evil" side of the tracks. Every day you put yourself in situations that confirm your self-diagnosis as a righteous non-rich individual. You unconsciously surround yourself with others who feel the same way, and all of you bombard each other constantly with messages about how right you are. The irony, however, is that you don't even know you are doing it to yourself. But you define yourself, and you choose your own economic situation. You're a self-programming robot.

Money Myth #3: By Opposing Wealth, You Become Pure

Everything that helps preserve the environment and uplift mankind is good; everything that destroys the Earth and harms mankind is evil and should be shunned. This is self-evident, right? Only the most self-serving maniac would disagree. Yet you continue to observe many people out there who do not feel this way: greedy individuals who dedicate themselves to raping others and pillaging the planet, and you rightfully categorize them as maniacs. They're insane. They're evil.

Certainly, these types of people exist: purely evil individuals with no social conscience or compassion for humanity. They are sociopaths, but there aren't many, and a good percentage of them are in prison or mental institutions. So, you look for other evildoers who must be out there spreading their wickedness, causing pain and misfortune. And voilà! You find them in the guise of profit-driven corporate leaders. But then you take your search one step further and get to know some of these corporate villains personally. To your surprise, you find that they are simply people trying to do their jobs and make a living. This happened when a group of Earth First protestors descended on the home of Sir Mark Moody-Stuart, then-chairman of Royal Dutch Shell. This CEO served tea to the dozen or so baffled young people and proceeded to tell them that he too cared for the environment and hoped that by working on the "inside" he would be able to do something about it.

But he really couldn't do much, could he? Even CEOs are pawns in the great struggle for dominion over the planet, its people and resources. Naturally, then, you began to look at the corporations themselves as the evildoers on the world's stage. As explained at length in the Canadian documentary, *The Corporation,* these huge companies exhibit all the personality traits of psychopathic maniacs, with no trace of a conscience. They are designed to achieve profit without heeding the cost to the environment or mankind, yet they are paradoxically protected by the laws of mankind.

Triumphant in your discovery, you deduce that corporations are the ultimate evil because they are all about profit; therefore, you conclude that profit itself must be evil.

The formula would look like this:

corporations = profit
AND corporations = evil
therefore, profit = evil

Do you see the faulty logic there? Using other parameters, I think you'll see what I mean:

bananas = yellow
AND bananas = fruit
therefore, yellow = fruit

That's right. Using your logic, everything yellow would be a fruit. Imagine the problems this logic would create for taxicab drivers.

Just because some corporations are bad does not mean that all money is evil. Yet somewhere deep in your psyche you equate money with evil, and you shun it. In order to uphold THE DEMAND FOR PURITY within yourself, you disassociate from anything that could be labeled "for profit."

Do you see how this might hamper your ability to ever *make* a profit in your life? No matter how often or how loudly you bemoan your moneyless state, you will always remain in that state as long as you continue to hold firmly to this internal disassociation.

And as you demand purity over profit for yourself, you let shame become a powerful guiding factor in your life. You have a deep abiding shame at the unfair and manipulative ways in which the world of economics works. You are secretly ashamed of yourself for your part in it, so you keep your distance from the main tool of shame, which, of course, is money. Instead, you associate yourself with supposedly shameless people, causes, and investments ("green" funds, for example, or fuel-efficient cars, natural fiber shirts, nonprofit organizations, struggling enterprises that do not make much profit, etc).

You also experience a lot of guilt because you cannot exist in the modern economy without taking part in some of its inequalities. We may protest global warming, for instance, but in order to make it to the protest site in another state, we drive to the airport, take a jet, and hop on a bus once we are there, gobbling up fossil fuels the whole time. On the way, we order food wrapped in plastic, which has been grown with chemical fertilizers. By definition, modern people are taking part in the modern economy, and we all feel a vague underlying guilt for taking part in what we perceive as an imperfect and ultimately harmful system. To punish ourselves, we make sure not to hoard "too much" money, which would prove our guilt as greedy profiteers. Instead, we always seem to accumulate just enough to "get by." Any more than that, and we lose it: We spend it; it's stolen; we give it away. It disappears as if by *magic.*

Money Myth #4: Liking the Things Money Can Buy Is a Weakness

One thing that you do to reinforce your membership in the cult of moneyless robots is to confess your weaknesses, impurities, and imperfections to yourself and to others in your situation on a regular basis. "I admit I love McDonald's hamburgers," you say. "I just can't help myself." Or, "I love to drive my gas-guzzling SUV. It's the one thing I can't give up. Besides, they're safer."

What is your "one thing"? The one thing you spend money on and blatantly show you can afford, even though you know it is "bad" for you or self-indulgent? Caffeine? Tobacco? Diamonds? Chocolate? Shoes? Clothes? It has to be something, because as a group member, you must by definition reveal your imperfections. This is THE CULT OF CONFESSION of the moneyless masses. You let everyone know you aspire to goodness, but always confess you fall short. You don't claim to be "perfect" (i.e., able to live without needing money), but you do in effect claim that a perfect version of you, a non-materialistic version, exists out there somewhere, but that you'll simply never reach it. You are, at your very core, not good enough.

Fiscal confession can be seen as a counterpart to keeping up with the Joneses. It's "staying down with the Joneses." If you are seen as rising too far above your peers and you let it be known, you have essentially joined another class—the class that has allowed money into their lives—and you have escaped the moneyless bubble. But you cannot do this until you change your self-concepts and self-definitions. That is why people who receive a windfall or win the lottery usually end up back in their financial comfort zone quite quickly, having lost or spent most of the money.

Having a large sum of money in your wallet or bank account does not mean you have Made the Switch to Being Rich. It only means that, for the moment, you have a large sum of money in your wallet or bank account. Being rich means something else. It means being free to do what you love to do. As Henry David Thoreau said, "Wealth is the ability to fully experience life." If you find yourself making excuses or needing to "confess" your weakness when you're enjoying the things money can buy, you are a believer in Myth #4.

Money Myth #5: Poverty Is Holy

There can be no questioning your integrity. Am I right? At the very least, people can look at you and say to themselves, "Well, she must be a good person because she certainly hasn't spent all her money on frivolous things and useless bling. She has substance. She's dedicated herself to her art, her mission, her cause. She's not superficial."

I'm not talking here about the holy poverty of a Saint Francis, though if you're like me, his example may be attractive to you. I once made a pilgrimage to Assisi and stood trembling with awe, gazing upon the little church of San Damiano, which Saint Francis repaired with his own hands. I have always spiritualized and romanticized poverty in my mind. You may want to look at your own list of heroes and see how many of them were poor artists who rose to great heights, or people of humble origins who became great leaders, or rich people who chose poverty as their path, such as Francis or Siddhartha Gautama who became the Buddha. Basically, anyone who put spirituality or "goodness" together with poverty or suffering. Gandhi comes to mind. Mother Theresa. Nelson Mandela. You get the idea. These heroes make poverty seem better than wealth. It's pure; it's spiritual; it's on a higher level.

You are part of a group that has a built-in belief in the holiness of poverty, and an intricate SACRED SCIENCE has been developed around this concept. But the poverty you believe in is only holy if it is chosen or risen above. The plain old nasty poverty that much of the world is forced to grind through on a daily basis is not what you think about when you think about poverty.

You think more highly of yourself because you believe that money does not matter. You think that a life of selflessness and holy artistic poverty is better than a life of striving for wealth. If, God forbid, you were to start focusing on making money, you would quickly start to feel guilty and ashamed. You would label yourself a "sell out."

Ultimately, you sabotage any of your own attempts at getting rich because you subconsciously believe that striving for money would make you unholy. This is not true, but a very precious part of your self-image is caught up in believing it is.

See, Robot? You're doing this to yourself. You're holding yourself captive in the prison of your own ideas. You are brainwashed.

Money Myth #6: You Could Have More Money If You Only Wanted It, but You Don't

The very words that come out of your mouth are making it impossible for you to achieve the monetary goals you claim to be striving toward. You do not need a cult leader standing by to censor your speech, because you are doing it to yourself.

"Sure, I could get rich if I really wanted to," you say. "I'm smart enough. I have great ideas. Plenty of people get rich every day. But why should I put in the effort? That's not what I've been put on the planet to do." Then, later, when you're alone in the dark of the night examining your life, that familiar sense of desperation creeps into your stomach because you're worrying about money again. The problem is that you do not have the words to express the fact that it's OK to have money.

You are LOADING THE LANGUAGE of your own failure. You use the "thought-terminating clichés" that Lifton spoke about to make life easier. These expressions quickly explain away any of the nasty complexities of the real world. As Lifton said, "The most far-reaching and complex of human problems are compressed into brief, highly reductive, definitive-sounding phrases, easily memorized and easily expressed."

"Oh, he's just a rich snob," you say. End of story.

"Money destroyed that family." "Let them eat cake." "Rich people are mostly miserable." "Ill-gotten gains." "Filthy lucre." "Poor little rich girl." "It takes money to make money." "The rich get richer and the poor get poorer." "He who dies with the most toys wins."

And of course the granddaddy of them all: "Money is the root of all evil."

You're talking yourself out of the very riches you claim that you want, Robot. When will you stop?

Money Myth #7: Money Would Change You

Far be it from you to suddenly get rich and begin expressing those aspects of yourself that you have politely kept out of the spotlight all this time. You believe, along with the other members of the money-less masses, that it is more important to do good humbly, just get by, and not ask too much from life. Who do you think you are, anyway?

Your character has been and continues to be shaped by your belief in the idea that money is essentially bad. Accordingly, you bury your stronger characteristics so that you avoid potential leadership roles and the fulfillment of your own secret vision of yourself as a rich powerful person. You believe that it is better to serve than to lead, better to give than receive, better to do anything rather than show off, which is what rich people do, right?

The problem is, you know who you are inside and it is a constant strain to cover up that powerful person, putting DOCTRINE OVER PERSON all the time, stifling yourself.

You think that if you suddenly became rich you would change. The evil tendencies of wealth would rub off on you. All of your visions for helping people, improving life on the planet, and expressing yourself through your talents would quickly fade away. You fear that you would become somebody else if you had money.

It is my belief, however, that you are *exactly* the type of person who should become rich, precisely because you are not likely to change.

By a certain age, people are who they are. You are already a helper, a giver, an artist, a humanitarian, an environmentalist. You care about people and the planet. You are precisely the type of person who *should* be rich, in order to have the resources to put your plans into action. By allowing a doctrine of intimidation to run your life and guide your decisions, you are not doing anybody any favors. Money will not change you into a bad person. In fact, from my point of view, by not becoming rich, you may be doing the world irreparable harm. Who knows what you could be accomplishing if you weren't allowing your fears to hold you back?

Money Myth #8: If You Became Rich, You Would Cease to Exist

If you examine yourself closely enough, you may actually glimpse the truth for a moment and understand that you are, believe it or not, in love with poverty. You're in love with the lore and lingo of the righteous moneyless masses. The thought of becoming a rich person frightens you. It would be like giving up a loved one, a member of your family. It would be like giving up your self.

The thought of becoming rich makes you feel almost as if the world would swallow you up whole. The heavy weight of wealth (of gold and houses and physical riches) would sink you where you stand, and you would cease to exist. Your self-concept as a non-rich person is responsible for DISPENSING YOUR EXISTENCE. In order for the "rich you" to be born, the "poor you" must die, and that is scary.

Without the comfortable level of economic limitations you've become used to, life would lose much of its meaning. What would you actually do with all that money? You wouldn't know what to think or how to act. It is not enough to simply have money. You have to learn how to be rich.

And, equally important, you subconsciously know that if you become rich you will no longer have the need for anyone else to tell you what to do. You will, in a sense, be your own boss, and that is a huge fear. What are you going to do with that kind of freedom? What will you do tomorrow morning if you don't have to report to anyone because you no longer need a job? Will you be capable of making your own decisions in life? What will people say when they see the life you have wrought when you have nobody else to blame? Can you be completely responsible for your own existence?

Up until now, the answer, most likely, has been no.

I know that you are still not convinced. Just like my mind did in that Denver basement, your mind is now scurrying desperately back into its shell, frantically covering itself up with old patterns regarding money so that you can remain faithful to the belief in yourself as a good, "saved" person who cares about the "important" things in life. You're uncomfortable with the direction this is going. Even now, I imagine you attempting to regain your sense of composure. You think all this talk about brainwashing and thought control is crazy, don't you?

As Ted Patrick said to me at the end of our first session, I say to you now, "That's right, Robot. Go ahead and smirk. This is just the beginning"

I slept on a single bed in one corner of the basement that night. The two strongmen were posted nearby, one by the stairs, one in the room next to me. When I got up late in the night to use the bathroom, they watched me closely, waiting for me to make another vain attempt at escape. My body was weakened from a diet low in protein; from the many nights in which I got no more than four hours sleep; from endless days and weeks spent roaming through suburbs and city centers begging for money, not a penny of which I would ever get to spend on myself or my family.

My father slept close by as well. I didn't have the slightest feeling of empathy for him or for the extreme stress he must have been under to attempt this crazy kidnapping. All I could think about was myself. Why was he doing this to me? I had made my decisions as an adult, and I wanted to be left alone to do whatever I wanted with my life. Why had my father hired this bully to push me down onto couches and persecute me with his talk about brainwashing? I wanted to stay exactly the way I was. I thought I had all the answers.

I did not sleep very well. I moved in and out of restless slumber and periods of half-awake anxiety. Cold air seeped in through cracks in the seals around the small, high windows as a December wind whistled outside. It was a long, dark night.

Chapter Three

The Seductions of Surrender

The next morning, as the sun rose and day two of my captivity in the Denver basement began, Ted Patrick was there waiting for me in his thick-lensed glasses with a serious look on his face, like he was ready to get down to business. He had his suit coat off and was dressed in a button-down shirt and slacks.

"Good morning, Robot."

That was getting old fast. I didn't say anything in reply.

My father emerged from his room looking sleepy and sheepish, like he didn't know exactly how all of this was supposed to proceed. The two strongmen slunk around in corners with that "I'd rather be outside smoking a cigarette" look on their faces. We all avoided each other's eyes.

"How about some breakfast?" suggested Patrick.

The door at the top of the stairs opened and the owner of the house descended carrying a tray of food. He was an older grizzly bear of a man, six-foot-four, bald, with a huge barrel chest. Apparently he was used to serving kidnapped guests breakfast in his basement. He said good morning, shot me a quick, kind glance, then disappeared back up the stairs.

"Eat up, Robot," said Patrick. "It's going to be a long day."

At first I didn't know what to do with all of the food heaped on the table. Before me was a spread of bacon, sausage, eggs, toast, bagels and cream cheese, fruit, pancakes, coffee, and juice. Steam rose from a stainless steel pitcher of coffee. To me, it looked like a spread fit for a king. I hadn't eaten any solid food before noon for months now, just smoothies in the morning, then the endless peanut butter and jelly sandwiches for lunch. Dinner was usually boiled vegetables and rice. Would it be right for me to indulge myself in this way? We were taught that we needed to purify ourselves and abstain from worldly pleasures in order to become truly spiritual people.

"What's wrong? Go ahead and dig in," said Patrick, obviously amused at my hesitation. I picked up a slippery wedge of pineapple from the plate and nibbled tentatively.

"That's not breakfast," said Patrick. "THIS is breakfast." He heaped food onto his plate, jumbling it all together, and dug in with relish, enjoying every bite. His two assistants did the same. Then my father joined them. They were all pouring syrup and spreading butter and slurping coffee. The bright blue sky outside the high window and the snow on the ground made the warm steamy food inside seem even more appetizing.

Suddenly, I realized how hungry I was. Not just regular hungry. Mega-hungry. Like I could eat everything on everyone's plate and then ask for seconds. Like I could keep eating for days.

Still, I held back. Patrick watched me out of the corner of his eyes while I slowly ate one slice of wheat toast and drank a glass of orange juice. After the plates were cleared away, Patrick got right to the point.

"Time to talk about that phony messiah of yours," he said.

"Excuse me?"

"You heard me, Robot. Let's talk about the so-called God-man, that guru of yours, 'Reverend' Moon. You're a Moonie, ain't ya? And proud of it, right? Well, tell me all about how wonderful he is. Come on."

Instead of pushing me down as he had the night before, he pulled up a chair right in front of mine and sat just inches away, staring at me expectantly, like he was genuinely interested in what I had to say.

"Well," I began, "he was a prisoner of war in a camp in Korea where he only got one tiny bowl of rice to eat a day. And he shared the bowl with other prisoners. Sometimes he gave them the whole thing."

"I don't want stories. I don't want hearsay that somebody told you. I want the facts. What do you actually know about this man? Were you there? Do you know for a fact that he ate only five grains of rice a day?"

How did Patrick know about the five grains? That was precisely the number we were told he had left in his bowl after giving his portion to his fellow prisoners. "No," I said hesitantly, "of course I wasn't there. I wasn't even born yet."

"So you're accepting all this on faith? You have faith in what they're telling you?"

"That's right."

"Nothing wrong with a little faith. But you're not allowed to question those 'facts,' are you? Nobody is allowed to question The Man."

He was right. We were never allowed to question. All of the stories and teachings had to be accepted at face value. But wasn't that the definition of faith? Believing what you couldn't prove? I liked having faith. So many of the people I'd known in my life had no faith in any-thing at all. Like my father, for example. What did he believe in? And these other men in the room? None of them had faith. I was differ-ent. I was stronger. I felt a smile spread out over my face.

"That's right, Robot. Go ahead and grin. But you're going to listen to what I have to say now, and you're gonna listen good." He grasped the arms of my chair and pulled it in closer to his so that our faces were almost touching. "Look at me now. That's it. I'm going to tell you a few things about your great guru, Moon."

And thus began my second lesson.

Patrick took out another book, *The Guru Papers*, by Joel Kramer and Diana Alstad, and handed it over to me. I flipped through the pages for a few moments and handed it back.

"What does this have to do with me?" I asked.

"These folks did a little research into how cults work and how people get controlled by gurus and other leaders. You know you're in a cult, right?"

"I am not in a cult," I replied. In my mind, I was following the one true leader of the world's one true religion. I certainly wasn't in any cult.

"Well, I'm going to tell you what these folks discovered when they looked into people who call themselves 'gurus,' which is exactly what your Moon is doing."

"That's ridiculous."

"Just listen."

Patrick then outlined the ten basic techniques used by gurus to control their followers. I tried to tune my mind out and recite mentally some of the chants and prayers I'd been taught in the Moonies, but every time Patrick noticed me doing this, he'd stop and pull his chair in even closer until I could smell the sausage and coffee on his breath.

The techniques used by gurus to control their followers include:

1. The Seductions of Surrender
2. The Assault on Reason
3. Maintaining Dominance
4. The Attractions of Hierarchy
5. Renunciation as Accumulation

6. Selflessness as Greed
7. Karma the Controller
8. Spiritual Permission
9. Converting Unbelievers
10. Deceit and Corruption

The Seductions of Surrender

Patrick explained that what people are looking for when they join a cult is a return to the sensation of being at the center of the universe. We all experienced it, if only for a short time, in infancy and early childhood, when we felt a sense of absolute rightness and were cared for by people who we thought had all the answers. It was a time of innocence and purity. Some people, especially those of us who are sensitive or compassionate, or spiritually inclined or artistically attuned, feel a grave sense of loss when we no longer experience this innocence and purity as adults, and we spend a good deal of time and energy seeking those sensations out again in one form or another.

When someone comes along and says "This is the path. If you follow me, you will attain enlightenment (or nirvana, or salvation, or oneness)," it is hard to resist their message. What their claims boil down to is that through obedience to their ideas and guidance, we will once again become whole, innocent, and pure. We will be saved. So we surrender to them in order to experience that.

"They told you that you had to 'surrender your attachments' to everything in your life except the guru," said Patrick. "Your belongings, your car, your cash . . . most members surrender everything. That's why they're so poor, and Moon's so rich. You know he's a multimillionaire, right?"

It was true. Revered Moon was extremely wealthy. But the Moonies had told me I had to give up worldly things like possessions, money, even family, in order to save my soul. Still, I didn't want to give Patrick the satisfaction of knowing he was right, so I kept quiet.

The Assault on Reason

"So," continued Patrick, "You've been giving up your so-called 'attachments' to all kinds of things, including your father here, am I right?"

I looked over at my Dad, who was hanging his head and looking forlornly at the floor.

Patrick continued his attack. "Do you think this man here in front of you, who raised you and cared for you and supported you, is just a thing you should 'surrender your attachment' to? Do you think that's reasonable?"

Once again I remained silent, but Patrick wouldn't let me.

"I'm a human being sitting right here in front of you, Robot. And your father is a human being, sitting right here, too. Human beings deserve respect. Talk to us now. Is it or is it not reasonable to 'surrender your attachment' to your own flesh and blood father?"

"I . . . don't know," I stammered.

"You don't know. Well, I know and let me tell ya, it's not reasonable. But this leader of yours makes you believe it is by feeding you all kinds of unreasonable, cockamamie stories. He's enlightened, right? He knows what's best for you, right? He's infallible, right? Then why did he marry an airline stewardess and claim she's a goddess? He can do anything he wants because he claims to live on a higher level than the rest of us mere mortals. But is that reasonable? No, it's an assault on reason. Look at the facts: He evades taxes. He gets arrested. He forces thousands of followers to work for peanuts while he lives in mansions. I'll tell you what he is. He's a slave driver who's controlling your mind but only because you're letting him."

Maintaining Dominance

"So how does he do this?" asked Patrick, not expecting me to answer. "I'll tell you how he maintains his dominance over you. First, he gets you to admit that you're not right. You're 'attached' to the wrong things. You do the wrong things. You can't trust yourself. Then he pits all you members against each other to see who can surrender the most and 'detach' the most from physical things. You get promised some special rewards if you can detach all the way and become like Moon himself. You might even live in the big mansion one day, if you're spiritual enough. But guess what, Robot? You're *never* going to be spiritual enough. It's all a big game to keep you members working against each other to sell the most flowers, make the most money for the group, and ask the fewest questions. The one thing you can never do is ask questions. Moon is 'enlightened.' He's above it all. And you have to swallow whatever kind of crazy story he tells you. All he has to do is act absolutely sure of himself, show no self-doubt, and he can do anything he wants to, because he's from a higher level. Am I right? Answer me now."

It was true. Moon's behaviors, his arrests, the fact that his own children had turned on him, his stewardess-wife, all of it was explained away as the actions of a man who operated on a level we could never hope to understand. All we could do is strive forever to try to attain that level ourselves. Would I ever get there?

"I don't know," I said again. They seemed like the only words I could utter.

The Attractions of Hierarchy

"You know why it felt so good to join that cult of yours?" asked Patrick. "It's because you suddenly didn't need to be in charge of your own life any more. It's tough being in charge, isn't it? You're expected to make all these decisions, all these career moves, and become this special person. But it isn't always so easy, is it? By joining the group, you get your choices made for you. They tell you where to go and what to do. And they tell you what's important in life, what to care about.

"It's a relief to give up your self-determination, because self-determination is hard. In its place you have competition within the group to see who can reach the highest level of detachment. And it's nice to know there's a big dog on top like Moon who's in control of everything and taking care of the big picture. What's most attractive about joining the group's hierarchy is you're no longer responsible for anything except taking orders. As long as you follow the plan, and the man in charge of the plan is blameless and perfect, you're blameless too."

Renunciation as Accumulation

"And the whole time you're getting detached from this and getting detached from that, you think you're becoming more and more holy, aren't you? You think other people are below you because they haven't given up their cars or their nice clothes, stereos, TVs, and jewelry. You're better than them, aren't you? All this so-called renunciation is really accumulation. But what you're accumulating isn't stuff, it's 'merit,' and all of you ambitious little Moonies are scrambling around like crazy trying to outdo yourself on the merit ladder."

Patrick stood up and paced back and forth, peering down at me each time he turned around in front of my chair in the cramped basement. My own arms and legs were aching, and I was dying to stand up and stretch also, but just as I started to ease my legs out Patrick sat back down and resumed his relentless grilling.

Selflessness as Greed

"I'm not saying you're a bad person," he continued. "You're probably a really nice guy. Most folks who join groups like that are fine people. But your niceness is being used against you. You wanna know how?"

He paused for a moment but when I didn't reply, he charged right back in. "Of course you wanna know how. This group is using your niceness against you by making you feel that it's wrong to be self-centered. They tell you it's egotistical to want what you want. That it's selfish to go after your own personal dreams; that you should be self-less instead. But guess what? The selflessness they're preaching is really just another form of greed. The harder you try to become self-less, which is unnatural anyway, the more self-centered you become.

"Every guru, including Moon, claims to be totally selfless, even though it's impossible to be totally selfless. It's the big lie. Selfishness is part of human nature. You're born into a body and mind as an individual, and that individual has wants and needs that are natural and normal. To try to get rid of them completely is a perversion of nature. The harder you try to destroy your 'ego' or whatever you want to call it, the more holier-than-thou you get. Do you think you're holier than I am? Come on, the truth."

I just stared at him.

"I said, 'DO YOU THINK YOU'RE HOLIER THAN I AM?'" He widened his eyes until I could see the whites all the way around the edges of his dark brown irises.

"I don't. . . ."

"Of *course* you do. You think you're holier than I am because you're following the one true God and doing all these selfless acts that make you better than the rest of us normal folk. But if you ask me, your selflessness is a kind of greed. A greed for feeling better than other people."

Karma the Controller

Suddenly, Patrick leaned back in his chair and curled his lips. It was the first time I'd seen him smile. "So, how's your karma doing?" he asked.

"What?"

"You heard me. Haven't you been building up a lot of 'good karma' through all your selflessness and sacrifice? How's it going?"

"I . . . don't know."

"Of course you don't know. You don't know because there's no way for people to know how their karma is doing. It's impossible. Karma is merit that's supposedly building up for you in some future life, and nobody can know how that life's gonna be 'till they get there. Moon is taking advantage of this whole karma concept to keep you all under control, constantly in fear that if you don't perform well now, you're going to ruin your chances for many lifetimes to come. All because of karma, the ultimate controller. It doesn't even matter that karma is an Eastern concept and the Moonies base their religion on Western Christianity. Moon uses the concept because it's such a powerful controller.

"There's some all-seeing force out there watching your every move, right? It's watching you right now to make sure you're being a good little Moonie and that you don't let big bad Ted Patrick lead you astray. That's right. I know what you're thinking, Robot."

Gradually, the smile faded from his face.

Spiritual Permission

Patrick leaned in close to me once more. "So, you're special. You're better than me. You're on some kind of spiritual mission. And everything you do while you're on that mission is OK. You've been given spiritual permission to do anything you want that serves Moon's interests. You can use heavenly deception as much as you want. You can say anything you want and do anything you want, as long as your lying and cheating are done for the group."

Patrick eyed me keenly. "What if," he said, "Moon gave you permission to hurt someone? Or even kill them?"

"I'd never do that."

"Really? Let me show you something else." He got up and went into another room, returning a moment later with a manuscript in his hands. "Do you recognize this?" he asked.

"No."

"Well, you should. This is the manual that Moon uses to train his more high-ranking followers. I want you to take a look at page 157, the part that I've underlined." He handed me the spiral-bound book. It was open to a page with one sentence highlighted by a yellow marker. What it said shocked me. I tried not to let the shock show on my face, but I couldn't help it.

"That's right, Robot. It says here that in order to be a true follower of Reverend Moon you have to be willing to kill your own parents."

"But that's never happened."

"How do you know it's never happened? Maybe you just never heard of it happening. Look at this man," he said pointing to my father. "Are you telling me that you'd be willing to kill him if Moon told you to?"

For the first time that day, my father spoke to me also. "Son," he said, "is it true?"

I had no answer for him.

Converting Unbelievers

"Tell me," said Patrick. "How many people have you 'witnessed' to so far?"

Apparently, he was familiar with this term also. "Witnessing" referred to our practice of going out onto the streets and asking people to come to one of our free dinners and listen to a lecture. It was the way we lured people into the group without telling them what we were all about up front.

"I'm not sure," I lied. "Maybe three or four." In reality, I knew I had witnessed to over a hundred people, and at least a dozen of them had accepted the invitation.

"It's probably more," said Patrick, "but anyway, that's part of what it means to be a cult member. You have to prove your loyalty by bringing in new members. And since you believe that you have all the answers to the world's questions, you actually think you're doing these folks a favor by tricking them into joining. Right?"

"We don't trick anybody. We just tell them what we believe and let people decide for themselves."

"Oh, I see. And when you first joined, for example, how long was it before anyone mentioned the name Reverend Moon to you or for that matter anything about God or a church of any kind?"

"I'm not sure," I lied again. "A few days maybe."

"It was probably several weeks. You were lured in with promises of happy group living. Let me ask you. Was the first Moonie to approach you a young woman?"

"Yes."

"And was she attractive?"

"I didn't notice."

"Liar!"

Deceit and Corruption

Patrick's sudden outburst startled me. I pulled back away from him in the chair, but he reached forward and grabbed me by both shoulders, shaking me the way you'd shake a sleeping person if you were trying to wake him up. "Of course you noticed!" he yelled. "You were a normal young man. It's OK to notice an attractive young lady."

He let go of me and slumped back into his chair. "I know it's hard to hear this, but you've got to listen to me now. Every last detail of Moon's grand plan is a lie. It's all a bunch of deceit and corruption. He's using you. He's using all of you. And it's not healthy. You should be out doing what young people do—going to school or working, going on dates, dancing, and having fun—but instead you spend all day running through parking lots selling flowers and living on peanut butter and jelly sandwiches so that Moon can live in his mansions. It's stunting your growth. It's warping you. Do you understand?"

For some reason, I started to shake violently, like I was freezing cold and shivering. I felt afraid of something, but I didn't know what it was.

"That's it," said Patrick. "You're listening to me now. You're hearing me. I can see it. Think about what I'm saying. Do you see how this group is keeping your mind under control? Do you see the techniques they've been using? They get you to surrender to them, and then they dominate you with all this talk about detachment and karma and selflessness. They tell you that this man Moon is a god. That he's completely selfless. But he's not. He's more attached than any of you. He's attached to the power that all your detachment creates. Everything you surrender, he gets, and that's addictive. His kind of power, based on lies, is like heroin for the soul. It has corrupted him, but you're not allowed to say that, or even think it, because he's supposed to be a saint, completely selfless. But I'll tell you who's really selfless. This man sitting next to you, your father, is selfless. He's the one who loves you and took care of you your whole life. Look at him now. Take a look."

I looked at my father. His eyes, I saw, were wet. He opened his mouth, like he wanted to say something to me, but then he closed it again. He seemed to be looking at me from far away.

"Look what you're doing to this man," said Patrick. "He's not perfect, like Moon claims to be, but he loves you. But instead of loving him back, you've surrendered your mind to this megalomaniac who's married to a stewardess and calls himself God. For just a moment here, do me a favor and think about what you're doing!"

I was shaking like a leaf now, slumping down in my chair. Patrick was watching me closely. Something was happening. My head felt heavy and filled with fog. I felt like I was going to pass out. Then, for a fleeting moment, I saw something. It was just a flash, but it was real. I saw that, just maybe, I had succumbed to the seductions of surrender that Patrick was talking about. What if it were true? What if I'd been duped by a group that cared more about controlling my mind than saving my soul? But then, in another flash, I forced those thoughts out of my mind and flipped instantly back into my faithful Moonie self. This fallen man wasn't about to trick me with all his talk about gurus and seduction. He could talk, but I didn't have to listen. I sat up straight in my chair again, staring past him over his shoulders.

Patrick sighed deeply and stood up. "You can run, Robot," he said, "but you can't hide. Not from me. We'll talk again later."

Chapter Four

*"Probably the greatest harm done by vast
wealth is the harm that we of moderate means
do ourselves when we let the vices of envy and
hatred enter deep into our own natures."*
Theodore Roosevelt

Money
of the Secrets
Millionaire
Gurus

A s far as money goes, you too are following a guru. You submit to his dominance and he controls all the cash. He exploits you for his own gain. You are intimately tied to this person who is running your financial life.

But who is he? To whom have you surrendered your mind? Who tells you how much money you should or should not have? Who is your Reverend Moon—your communist captor force-feeding you the information that is brainwashing you into your state of perpetual poverty? Who exactly is keeping you stuck in this moneyless bubble?

At first you may think it's a parent or other relative. Perhaps, it's an older sibling; a favorite teacher; your first boss; a girlfriend or boyfriend; a husband, wife, or lover. You may believe it's a friend who did the job. Or a group of friends. Peer pressure is strong, after all.

Any group you have belonged to, either peripherally or as a member, could have influenced you. And certainly TV, radio, magazines, and popular culture have a share in the blame, right?

Look deeper.

There is one key figure, one pivotal person, who through a kind of mystical manipulation has become the overriding influence in your life. Look closely in the mirror and you will see this phantom hiding there, peering out from the depths of your own eyes. It is so deep inside you—so inextricably linked with your self-image and what comprises the superstructure of your personality—that it will take superhuman effort to pry the poltergeist out.

The guru is you. Not the real you, but a false construction that has built up in your psyche over the years. You've internalized the controlling forces that maintain your present state of mind. This inner guru is the one keeping money out of your hands and putting it into the hands of others. And this guru makes sure you adhere to the rules of the moneyless masses.

Without knowing it, your subconscious mind has been using the same techniques that gurus use to keep their followers in a state of poverty. To counteract this conditioning, you must escape the

#	MONEY SECRETS OF THE MILLIONAIRE GURUS	CORRESPONDING CONTROL TECHNIQUE
1	YOU WANT TO BE DEPENDENT ON SOMEONE ELSE.	THE SEDUCTIONS OF SURRENDER
2	WHEN YOU ARE CONFUSED, YOU ARE EASY TO MANIPULATE.	THE ASSAULT ON REASON
3	YOU DON'T TRULY TRUST YOURSELF.	MAINTAINING DOMINANCE
4	YOU BELIEVE IN KINGS AND MOGULS.	THE ATTRACTIONS OF HIERARCHY
5	YOU ARE ADDICTED TO BEING GOOD.	RENUNCIATION AS ACCUMULATION
6	YOU ARE GREEDY.	SELFLESSNESS AS GREED
7	YOU'RE ON REMOTE CONTROL.	KARMA THE CONTROLLER
8	YOU THINK BEING POOR MAKES YOU SPECIAL.	SPIRITUAL PERMISSION
9	YOU WANT OTHERS TO BE POOR WITH YOU.	CONVERTING UNBELIEVERS
10	YOU ARE CORRUPTIBLE.	DECEIT AND CORRUPTION

control of this inner tyrant. You've got to deprogram the way your mind works . . . but how?

Well, all you need to do for now is listen. In this chapter, I'm going to explain the ten secrets that millionaire gurus know about their followers. They are the same secrets that you unknowingly use to control yourself and keep yourself from getting rich.

Money Secret #1: You Want to Be Dependent on Someone Else

Gurus know that on a subconscious level their followers want someone else to be in control. This is, perhaps, their most powerful secret. And in order to assert that control, all the guru must do is tell people what they want to hear in a tone of absolute certainty. He has to supply answers. It does not matter if these answers are right or wrong, true or false. If they are presented as being absolutely true, they create a sense of relief and happiness for those who believe in them. Believers no longer have to puzzle out the answers to life's questions. The answers are supplied automatically.

In a similar way, not being in charge of making your own money brings with it a return to the state of dependence and surrender you experienced as a young child. To re-create this state, you let others decide how much money you can have: your boss, your company, the government, the wealthy. You put yourself under the control of the people and institutions that do have money. You let them take care of things.

You are being SEDUCED INTO SURRENDERING to the idea that somebody "out there" can create security for you by supplying money in exchange for work. This idea is false.

The truth is that you can take back control of your life but only if you are willing to live with the uncertainty that comes with being in positions of power and control. You have to give up being coddled and step into the storm.

Have you ever noticed how most businesses—even those that appear well-run from the outside—seem to function chaotically? That things seem to run haphazardly and happen by chance? That the person in charge is barely getting by, flying by the seat of his or her pants? "How," you think to yourself, "do these people manage to be so successful and make so much money when they don't even seem to know what they're doing? I could do better than that."

But do you? That is the question. Control (and much of the wealth of the world) is reserved for the people who act: those who are willing to let go of the need to surrender to somebody else's control.

Your life, to a large degree, is determined by the roles you choose. Gurus, by definition, choose the role of "knower." All they have to do is act as if they know. Cult members, on the other hand, are by definition "seekers." Gurus know that if they don't offer seekers a sense of certainty, somebody else will.

This holds true in the realm of money as well. There is no absolute knowledge about finances. Wealthy or powerful people often have no idea what they are doing. But they assume the stance of someone who knows. They grow up and stop being seduced into believing that somebody else will take care of them.

Money Secret #2: When You Are Confused, You Are Easy to Manipulate

Gurus go to great lengths to confuse their followers. Even though they say they are trying to explain things clearly and make their teachings simple, in reality they pepper their speech with paradoxes and riddles. Why? In order to keep control and create an environment in which the followers cannot possibly be "right."

"No matter what position you take," say Kramer and Alstad in *The Guru Papers,* "you are always shown to be missing the point; the point being that the guru knows something you do not."

Have you ever listened to Allen Greenspan talk? Or the pundits who appear on MSNBC? Or any other economic gurus? Have you ever tried to read a corporate annual report or understand the complexities of the tax code? If you're a person who is more interested in people than numbers, chances are high that you got turned off very quickly. You may have felt that you had more important things to do with your time. You wanted to follow your passion, not dwell on boring details. And yet, there was also a part of you that felt inadequate and unintelligent when you compared yourself to people who could comprehend the intricacies of finance. Paradoxically, you felt "above it all" and "not good enough" at the same time. This is the ASSAULT ON REASON that keeps you feeling incapable of getting a firm grasp on your financial life.

Have you ever uttered the phrase, "Do what you love and the money will follow?" Have you ever thought it through? How, exactly, will the money follow? By magic? Will it simply appear from thin air? Probably not. It is with this kind of paradoxical thinking that you keep yourself confused and muddling along through your economic life. You are lowering the power of your reasoning faculties. You are keeping yourself uninformed and confused.

Money Secret #3: You Don't Truly Trust Yourself

Gurus know that inside each of their followers is a place of deeply embedded self-doubt. This self-doubt is sometimes created by early religious teachings that stress essential impurity or sinfulness. Parents, caregivers, and a wider culture stress uniformity and conformity as opposed to creative play. Today, three-year-old children are dressed in uniforms and supervised by adults in serious athletic contests, instead of being left to play and learn from each other. We are taught not to trust our own instincts and desires.

You don't trust yourself with money, either. As someone who cares more about the "important" things in life, you distrust your own desires for material goods and the things money can buy because they are "base," "lower," or "unspiritual." Yet, at the same time, you know that you want these things. You're a human being, after all, and you crave the things human beings crave: nice things, beautiful things, functional things, luxurious things. These desires create a schism in your mind, a tug-of-war between your "good" self and "bad" self. Part of you doesn't want to admit that the other part wants what it wants. You don't trust that part of yourself. In a sense, you don't trust yourself at all. How could you be so superficial? You know those diamonds are mined at the expense of poor people in other countries, yet you want them. You know that sports car is an extravagance that pollutes the environment, yet you crave it.

You have not fully accepted the part of yourself that craves. You put yourself down, judge yourself, and in the end do not trust yourself with your own money. You secretly feel that if you had lots of money you'd blow it on worthless material things. So you let others have the money. This is the way your moneyless self MAINTAINS DOMINANCE over your life.

Money Secret #4: You Believe in Kings and Moguls

Gurus offer people the chance to idolize somebody, to hold them to a higher standard. Because they are thought to be "enlightened," gurus are supposedly beyond self-interest and blame. Their followers hope to one day be like them, but in the meantime they believe that they are not like them. They believe only somebody else can be pure and blameless—somebody on a higher level. What these followers are actually doing is externalizing the blameless parts of their own natures, and in this manner they give a large percentage of their self-confidence over to somebody else.

Regarding money, this is the same dynamic at work in your own mind. Unconsciously, you elevate the rich and famous to a higher level and consider them somehow blameless and "better" than normal people. You cannot help yourself. It has been part of human nature for millennia to lift certain individuals up above the rest in terms of power and perfection, as attested to by the long line of purportedly "perfect" pharaohs, emperors, monarchs, and human gods who have lived and ruled throughout history. You believe in kings and moguls. It's in your blood.

You may think you are a rebel who despises kings and moguls, but the authoritarian belief system embedded in your mind functions perfectly nonetheless. The most common age at which people rebel is adolescence, yet what's the first thing adolescents do when they rebel against those in control? They choose another ruler, another idol, another person on a higher level. These are usually movie stars, athletes, singers, celebrities, or other rich and powerful icons. You do the same thing when you rebel against the rich. A part of you still wants them to have money, more money than you do, so that you can transfer onto them your own inner feelings of being "above it all" and blameless. Your mind tricks you into thinking they're different than you and that they exist on a higher level. They are not. Yet this conditioning is extremely powerful. You can tell yourself a million times that famous people are the same as you are, but if one walked through the door right now you would probably feel differently. Being in the presence of a famous person would undoubtedly have an impact, just as the guru does on his disciples' lives. Because of our deep programming over millennia, human minds create this authoritarian hierarchical structure that is difficult to dismantle. But you need to begin dismantling it, which is what this book will help you do.

The flip side of the equation is also true. At the same time that you believe certain people are on a higher level, you also believe others, including yourself, are on a lower one. And you believe that is where you belong. Someone from the moneyless masses who tries to prove her blamelessness is despised as a show-off. But someone who is at the guru level is assumed to be blameless, in spite of vast evidence to the contrary, as we discussed in Money Myth #4.

You are playing a game of follow-the-leader with the kings and moguls of the world, and they can treat you as they please. They can *make you feel shameful about not having money—it's a reflection of your lack of self-worth*—while they move in front of you, blameless and wealthy. Paradoxically these same people make you feel shameful about wanting money. They claim to be beyond the striving that they know you still experience. Do you ever get the feeling, when you're around wealthy people, that it was all just so easy for them? That it was a natural progression of events that led them to their riches and that the path for you is completely inscrutable? This is because your mind is putting them on another level.

By letting those with money—the bosses, corporations, and institutions—control your thinking, you're giving up the self-determination (and challenges) that would come with creating your own business and life. This is THE ATTRACTIONS OF HIERARCHY. Their wealth gives you an excuse for not doing what you know you could be doing. Your own wealth would lift you out of the realm of excuses. As Kramer and Alstad said in The Guru Papers, "A necessary element in becoming an adult is realizing that ultimately others cannot know what's best for you."

You have a co-dependent relationship with the rich and famous of the world. You keep them on their level, and you keep yourself on yours. Where does that leave you, Robot? Often, I would bet, it leaves you in a secret state of negative emotions.

But the hierarchy, unfortunately, is built into your brain. You are hardwired into placing yourself beneath some great, wealthy leader in the chain of command. How are you ever going to escape?

Money Secret #5: You Are Addicted to Being Good

Gurus know that their followers are eager to earn brownie points on the spiritual hierarchy they have created. These points are gained through any act dedicated to the group rather than to the individual. These acts are labeled as "good."

You do the same thing when it comes to money. The more good you do (the more free time you give up, the more committees, boards, and associations you volunteer for, etc.), the higher your standing among your non-materialistic peers. You are expected to do your part and not ask for rewards. You experience your RENUNCIATION AS ACCUMULATION, because you are accumulating merit. Your actions are adding to your spiritual worth, not your net worth, and that is much more important to you. In fact, you will often shun activities that would add to your net worth because you perceive them as being opposed to your spiritual worth. You mistakenly label one thing as the opposite of the other.

Do you feel a sense of being "better" than those people who focus on money? Then you are, perhaps unconsciously, accumulating merit in your own mind for the things you are giving up. The two main items you give up are your time and money (the money you could have made if you'd focused on that instead). This is where you acquire your sense of self-worth. It's where you feel wealthy. It's what makes you feel good—a sensation you're addicted to—and you'll do anything in your power to keep those feelings flowing. The most obvious thing you do is keep avoiding money. So, even though you say you'd like more money, you push it away at the same time.

Money Secret #6: You Are Greedy

Gurus know something about their followers that the followers themselves are afraid to admit: They're greedy. In fact, they are often more greedy than so-called "materialistic" people. They are not necessarily greedy for material things, but often their ambitions are extremely intense. These ambitions are cloaked, however, behind a veil of selflessness and holiness. Gurus can use their followers' greediness to manipulate them and get them to do almost anything, whether or not it's in their followers' best interests.

Are you a win/win person? Someone who doesn't love competition? Someone who wants everyone to come out on top? It is good to want the best for others, but chances are high that you are unfairly denying the competitive part of your own nature. What you may actually be doing is substituting one kind of competitiveness for another. You compete to be selfless. You compete to most effectively save the Earth, heal other people, take care of the world's problems, or develop interesting, creative projects that will demonstrate your deeply spiritual outlook on life.

All of this is masking pure raw ambition. It is masking your greed. And you cannot admit it to yourself or anyone else because that would destroy your self-image as a good, spiritual person. In fact, there is a good chance that you do not even know how greedy you are. You have masked it even from yourself, refusing to consider your SELFLESSNESS AS GREED, but that is partly what it is. Only after you have unmasked this aspect of your psyche will you be able to channel your natural selfishness to a more appropriate end. You'll be able to stop hiding your ambition behind a veil of purity.

But how will you accomplish this?

Money Secret #7: You're on Remote Control

Gurus know they don't have to be present in order to control their followers. In fact, they never even have to meet them. I never met Reverend Moon in person. Many followers have only the most fleeting of face-to-face encounters with their leader. It is not physical presence that controls people, but doctrine passed down through a hierarchy of authoritarian control.

In terms of money, nobody needs to stand over you and remind you to keep yourself poor. You're following orders from afar. You're on remote control. But where did those orders come from?

If you are a "spiritual" person, or if you work in the helping and creative professions, regardless of your religious affiliations, you quite likely feel a kinship with the Eastern concept of karma. You have come to believe that some invisible, often spiritual, force is at work behind the scenes in your life and that if you pay heed to its rules, you'll end up much better off. KARMA THE CONTROLLER is controlling you from afar.

Have you ever seen karma? Have you ever seen a past or future life? Really seen it? The answer is no. You may have seen something inside your own mind that you took to be another life, but what you were experiencing was something in this life. And chances are good that you didn't see anything but merely adapted the familiar phraseology of karmic thinking as it was passed down to you by writers, teachers, or friends.

How many times have you heard the phrase, "It must be her karma," or something along those lines and not given it a second thought? We "good" people in the West have fully bought into this Eastern concept. You may have felt secretly rebellious and avant-garde for believing in this non-traditional concept, but karma is anything but avant-garde. It is Eastern religions' most powerful authoritarian tool. It is not a specific code of behaviors, but rather one overarching abstract rule that can be summed up in five words: "You get what you deserve."

In your case, you deserve to have little money. It must have been something you did in a past life. At the same time, you had better continue to do good and focus on helping others, rather than helping yourself to more riches, because if you do not follow the rules of this invisible energy, you doom yourself to pain and suffering at some future time. And if you do not experience the pain and suffering in this life, don't worry—it will catch up to you sooner or later. There is no way to outsmart the law of karma. It is one of the most powerful control techniques on the planet. It has kept countless millions trapped in caste systems and millions of others trapped in lives of self-imposed limitation.

Western tradition also incorporates some of this karmic thinking. Have you heard the Bible quote, "It is easier for a camel to pass through the eye of a needle than it is for a rich man to enter the kingdom of God?" Obviously, this man was not thinking the right thoughts or performing the right actions. He was focused on material things; because of that, he developed bad karma. Because he was thinking about money, he was denied the presence of God. How horrible is that?

You will never come face to face with the powerful leader who is keeping you locked in your financial situation. There is no leader. There is only a system. A concept. And this concept is controlling your every action. You have got to think your way out of this conceptual box, but unfortunately it is your very thought process that is keeping you inside of it.

How are you ever going to change your thoughts?

Money Secret #8: You Think Being Poor Makes You Special

Gurus know that if their followers think of themselves as special and above the rules that apply to other people, they can be convinced to do almost anything. Their "higher purpose" gives them SPIRITUAL PERMISSION to do whatever is necessary to achieve their goals.

As long as you continue to define yourself as a "good" person as opposed to a "rich" person, you feel you have permission to do whatever you need to do to achieve your goals. You have to go to work. You have to make money. You have to do what your boss says. But if you became wealthy, you would no longer need to work to make money. You would have money. You would no longer have a boss to tell you what to do and schedule your life for you. You would be the boss. If you were to become wealthy, everything you do would become a choice, not an obligation. You would no longer be able to make excuses.

You also feel that if you begin focusing on money, you would lose focus on your ideals and you would no longer be special. You fear that becoming rich would make you ordinary.

So you keep yourself poor and special. You choose to be one of those people who struggle for a living because you believe it is noble.

Meanwhile, the guru sits back and lets his followers play their noble games while he takes all their assets.

Money Secret #9: You Want Others to Be Poor with You

Gurus convince their followers that it's important to CONVERT UN-BELIEVERS to their point of view. Since the group's philosophy is cutting-edge and the "correct" reality, anyone not following the program is missing out on a great opportunity. Converting unbelievers is in their best interest.

You too feel that others would benefit by being inside the same moneyless bubble you're in. So, in many subtle ways, you are always ready to convert people to your point of view. It's in the words you speak, the clothes you wear, the car you drive, and the products you buy. You're always putting a message out: It's cool to not be rich.

You don't feel right unless you're surrounded by other people who share your belief in the impurity of money. You're part of a group of like-minded individuals, and all of you are reinforcing your status in the world because this group is the "right" one, the "best" one.

"Other" people are rich. You and the people in your group are good and spiritual, helpful and artistic, and you work hard on the important things in life, not on accumulating cash. The more friends and believers you gather around you, the better you feel about your own financial situation. Aren't your friends wonderful? Don't they each have an interesting story to tell? Aren't you glad they've joined your group and haven't sold their souls for money? Aren't they more honest and worthy than the people in ritzier neighborhoods who think about nothing but money? By applauding their lack of materialism, you're helping keep them honest.

And you're all helping to keep each other poor.

Money Secret #10: You Are Corruptible

Gurus like their followers to believe in a strange fairy tale. Perhaps they even believe in it themselves. The story goes like this: "I am perfect (or near perfect, or chosen by God), and I am here to lead you all toward higher levels of awareness and, eventually, salvation. I am beyond all attachments. Everything I do is inspired by deep insights into the nature of life. Follow me, and I will help you achieve this state, too."

The problem is that this story, like all fairy tales, is not true. Gurus are human, just like you and me. What gurus are really doing is using an authoritarian hierarchy to deceive their followers and further their own self-interests. The whole relationship is based on DECEIT AND CORRUPTION.

You also believe in a fairy tale. Your story goes like this: "I am a good, spiritual, compassionate, artistic, helpful person, and my reason for being here is to help others lead the best life they can. Everything I do is inspired by my basic nature, which is focused on helping, not on making money. As long as I stay true to this philosophy, I can do no wrong."

But this too is a lie. It is a fairy tale. The truth is that you are human; therefore, your very nature is corruptible. Given the right circumstances, you would take advantage of others for your own personal gain. So, you purposely keep yourself on the bottom of the authoritarian hierarchy in order to avoid that possibility. By continuing to think and act like a good person who is not interested in money, you are successfully avoiding this temptation. You keep yourself poor to avoid the temptations of being rich.

If asked about this, however, you would deny everything. In your mind, you are simply being "good." This is how you have been programmed to feel.

But who is doing the programming? And when will you wake up to the fact that the person in control is not you?

After lunch, Patrick sat me back down for another session, and for three more hours we went over the same ground we had already covered. I could tell he was getting tired. His normally bright brown eyes were a little glazed behind his thick glasses. I'd overheard some of his conversations with my father and the others in the basement, and I had the impression that he was a very busy man. There were other captives, apparently, in other basements in cities around the country, all awaiting their encounters with Mr. Patrick. He had a large network of assistants stretched from coast to coast.

At first I was a little annoyed that he didn't seem to be so interested in me anymore. I felt like he was dismissing me, and for some strange reason I wanted his full attention, the full weight of his opposition to me. If he didn't care enough to put up his best fight, then I had already won.

The whole thing was getting a little boring, and during the late afternoon I gradually began to feel more confident. Patrick had run out of ammunition. He had used every trick in his book, and failed. I was still 100 percent faithful. All of his arguments, though interesting, had done nothing to change me.

Patrick left before dinner, heading up the stairs and out into the cold Denver dark. The others, including my father, left me alone. I had the impression that they didn't know what to do with me, how to treat me, or what to say to me when Patrick wasn't there. What do you say to a mindless robot? I left them sitting around the little table in silence and crawled into my single bed, pulling the covers up over my face.

I went to sleep early and as I drifted off, I tried to imagine what Ted Patrick was doing at that moment. Was he listening to jazz? Drinking bourbon and beer? He was obviously a fallen person who would never in a million years understand my spiritual dedication. Maybe he had given up on me. He was out getting drunk, and he was not coming back. I was saved.

But little did I know what he had in store for me next.

Chapter Five

"Authoritarian methods do not produce independence: they reinforce dependence."
Elaine Heffner

Gorillas and Wild Horses

After breakfast the next morning there was still no sign of Ted Patrick. Maybe he really had given up. Without him there, I took the opportunity to eat a full bowl of cereal, two slices of buttered toast, some fruit and yogurt. I didn't care if my father and the others saw me eat. For some reason, Ted Patrick was the one I wanted to impress with my faith and self-sacrifice. He was the one watching me. Judging.

It wasn't a Patrick-sized breakfast, but it was still satisfying. I thought I could actually feel the extra nutrition streaming through my veins. After I ate, I paced in circles around the small basement while my father and Patrick's two assistants sat at the table talking in low tones, gingerly avoiding eye contact, as if I were a rare and fragile species of animal that could be easily spooked.

By mid-morning I was on the bed again, half-dozing. I felt bored and restless. They'd tried their best to deprogram me, but it had obviously failed. I was proud of myself, but at the same time I was suspicious. It was almost too easy. And my pride was hurt. Were those other clients on Patrick's list, in other cities, really more important than I was?

Suddenly, the door at the top of the stairs flung open, and he stomped down into the basement. He didn't look as though he'd been drinking bourbon all night. In fact, he looked stronger and more vibrant than when I'd first met him. Still finely dressed in suit and tie, he nonetheless had the unmistakable air of an athlete.

"Ready for another day!" he chirped to nobody in particular. "It's gonna be a good one. I can feel it. Come on over here, Robot."

Here we go again, I thought. More ridiculous books and endless lectures. Well, no matter how many sermons he threw at me, I wasn't going to budge. I'd learned my lesson. I'd just humor him, pretend to listen to his ideas, let my lower lip tremble a little, as if I were scared and about to change my mind, but it would all be an act. I'd never change my mind or lose my faith. I knew how to play this game now.

I got up from the bed and trudged over to the chair, slumping down again, preparing myself for another round of interrogation.

"What's wrong?" asked Patrick. "You look a little weak this morning. Come on, let's flex our muscles a little. Get the blood moving. Let's get real."

With that, he stripped his coat off, undid his tie, adjusted his belt, and placed his hands on his hips, like a football coach. "Hit the deck," he said. "Give me twenty."

"Excuse me?"

"You heard me. Drop to the ground and give me twenty pushups. Twenty is nothing for a young man. I'm more than twice your age and I bet you I can do more pushups than you can."

"You've got to be kidding."

"No, I'm not kidding. I'll show you. Come on. Let's tussle."

He roughed up my hair, but it was done affectionately, not in an abusive way. Clearing tables and chairs out of the way in the cramped basement, he dropped down gracefully in one fluid movement and began doing pushups, counting out loud.

"One, two, three, four . . ."

They were good pushups, not the cheating kind when you only bend your elbows half way. His big chest brushed the worn carpet each time, and his arms locked when he came up, grunting out the next number. "Twenty-two, twenty-three, twenty-four . . ."

He went on and on. It was amazing for a man his age. Finally, he began to slow down. "Forty-five, forty-six, forty-seven . . ."

Finally, he let out a sigh and collapsed onto his stomach on the carpet. "Forty-eight," he gasped. He breathed heavily for a minute before standing back up again. "Not bad, eh, Robot? Now it's your turn." I hesitated. "Come on, now. Don't be afraid to show me what you're made of. I'm 48 years old, and I did my age in pushups. Let's see if you can do the same."

For six months I hadn't done any exercise at all. Though I had always been in decent shape before joining the Moonies, I had let myself go.

"Come on," Patrick cajoled me. "That's only nineteen pushups. You're not telling me you can't do nineteen lousy pushups, are you?"

His badgering finally got to me. I'd show him. Just because I was a spiritual person who had dedicated himself to a worthy cause didn't mean I was a wimp. I bent over, placed my palms on the carpet, and started to push.

"That's it. More! More!" shouted Patrick. He was actually cheering me on.

Six, seven, eight.

It was much harder than I thought it was going to be. In high school I'd been able to do fifty pushups and not even get out of breath. I was on the wrestling team and the track team. What was going on?

Thirteen, fourteen, fifteen.

My arms were trembling. They were jelly. I wasn't going to make it.

"Come on," yelled Patrick. "All the way up. No cheating."

Seventeen . . .

"Umphh." I hit the floor with a thud. Seventeen pushups. What a disgrace.

Patrick reached down and supported me under my arms, helping me stand again. I didn't look at him. It was embarrassing. I was weak. Outdone by a middle-aged man, when I was nineteen and supposedly at the pinnacle of strength and virility. Suddenly, my lack of virility started to worry me. I hadn't felt sexually stimulated in months. It was almost as if my hormones were dormant, including testosterone and the growth hormone that would make my muscles stronger. What was happening to me?

"Here, have a drink," said Patrick. He handed me a glass of orange juice as I sat down in the chair again. I drank for a moment in silence. Then Patrick placed a strong black hand on my soft white back. "It's OK, son," he said. "With a little more workin' out you'll whup me. I can see you're a strong young man."

It was weird, but when he called me son, I felt like crying. Patrick pulled up a chair and sat across from me, just inches away once again.

"Do you feel like you want to impress me? Like what I think about you is important?" His voice was soft and kind.

I was mute.

"I thought so," he said. "That's the way it works. It's natural. Would you like me to tell you what I'm doing to you here?"

"What you're doing to me?"

"That's right. I'm using a technique here to help deprogram you."

I couldn't believe he was being so upfront about it. I looked him in the eye.

"Basically, I'm establishing myself as the new alpha male in your life," he said. "Right now, Moon is your alpha male. You've surrendered yourself to this hierarchy of his. You've submitted. He dominates you. I'm just taking over some of that role now so you'll do what I say instead of what he says. It's like gorillas and wild horses."

"Like what?"

"Most people live like a pack of wild animals—gorillas and wild horses—following the alpha male, the silverback gorilla or wild stallion. They're stuck in a structure, completely dominated by their leader. People are even worse than animals really, because at least animals submit to a leader who's standing right in front of them, someone who's intimidating them right to their faces, not to some pie-in-the-sky guru who says he's better than you from afar and gets you dancing on a string with his manipulations of guilt and shame." He paused for a moment, staring off into space. Then he looked back at me.

"This is what's happening to you. It's not a pretty picture. You're submitting to a male-dominated authoritarian structure. Like a lot of the worst ideas of the past two thousand years, it's a paternal, hierarchical load of crap. But don't feel too bad."

"Why shouldn't I?"

"Because you're not alone."

Patrick and I talked and talked that day, but it was less like a one-way lecture now. More like a two-way conversation. His words were sinking in. And they sink in now as I contemplate how we are all played, like "puppets on a string," when it comes to our money.

Somebody "out there," some power figure—the secretary of the treasury, the president of the United States, the head of the world bank, the CEO of the corporation, the owner of your company, your landlord, boss, or supervisor—is holding the reigns, and you are being ridden. You're a beast of burden, forced to run after a limited amount of cash that will never be enough. Why is this so?

You allow yourself to remain in this submissive situation because it makes you feel more at ease. It creates a false sense of security by erasing your doubts about the state of the world. Just as people turn to structured religious or political groups to gain a sense of certainty regarding the meaning of life, you turn to a hierarchical structure to gain a sense of certainty regarding your financial life. It is too scary to go through life (and approach death) believing there is nothing but a void out there. So you let others tell you the way things are. You follow the lead of the alpha male, somebody with an answer. And, similarly, it is just too scary to go through life believing nobody but you has control over your financial destiny. So you position yourself within a monetary hierarchy with somebody else in charge.

The awful, scary truth is that nobody else has all the answers. Nobody knows better than you what is best for you. Certain people, though, stand in the posture of authority, and you let them. You insist on sticking to the old authoritarian way of structuring your life. You put somebody else in control. This is a reflexive action. Your natural response to the scary truth is to want to be consoled, to be told by someone of authority that everything is OK. Usually that person is male. The power structure is paternalistic. You, being a healer, teacher, artist, or caretaker claim to have a more maternal, feminine, goddess-centered point of view. Yet you submit, nonetheless, to the silverbacks of the world.

How can you break free?

Patrick tried hard to break me free of my own submissive tendencies, chipping away at my defenses all afternoon long. That evening, we all ate a big spaghetti and meatball dinner together, and I had two helpings.

Afterwards, when the dishes were cleared away, Ted Patrick turned to my father and said, "I think he's almost ready. He's getting there now. Take a look at him."

I didn't know what he was talking about. I was still a Moonie, still a fierce believer. But there was a shiver of fear in me, too. I was shaking again, like a butterfly vibrating within a cocoon before breaking free. What did he mean, I was almost ready? Why were they all looking at me that way? What was that glint of hope in my father's eyes?

I pushed back from the table and hurried into the bathroom, locking myself in. Quickly, I scanned the room.

"It's no use, Robot," came Patrick's voice from outside the door. "The window's been screwed shut from the outside."

Of course, I still tried it. The window was solid as a rock. It wouldn't budge. And it was so small and high up that I probably wouldn't have been able to escape through it anyway. Finally, I gave up.

Sitting down on the closed toilet seat, I had a strange argument with myself. It was as if there were two Steves: the Moonie Steve and the non-Moonie Steve. But how could that be? I'd made up my mind. I was dedicated. I was pure. Why had I allowed myself to eat all that food and sit there all day actually listening to what Patrick said? I was being weak. There were not two Steves, just one impure Moonie behaving badly.

Rocking back and forth in the bathroom, I began to chant to myself silently, so that the others couldn't hear me. "Heavenly Father, help me through this trial. I'm impure. Please save me." Over and over again I said it, until I began to feel sick.

Whirling around, I flung the toilet seat open and vomited into the bowl, purging myself of the day's excess. Afterwards, I spent another ten minutes chanting to myself while the voices outside the door grew steadily more insistent.

"Are you OK in there? It's time to come out now. Don't make us break the door down."

I took a deep breath and looked into the mirror. There, staring back at me, was my shiny-eyed, unconquerable Moonie self. I was ready.

Opening the door, I stepped out into the room. My father's whole face dropped. His earlier hope evaporated instantly when he saw me.

I walked over to the single bed without saying a word to anyone and curled up under the covers.

In the middle of the night I felt a presence sink down onto the thin mattress, and I opened my eyes.

"Dad?" He was sitting there just staring at me, with tears in his eyes and a look of terror on his face.

"Is it true?" he asked in a whisper.

"Is what true?"

"Would you really kill your mom or me if you were asked to? How could that be? We're a close family. We love you."

I was silent. He was obviously in pain, but there was nothing I could say or do to help him. He just didn't understand. None of them did. None of them saw how important it was for me to believe in something. I didn't want him to think I would ever hurt him, though. I loved him, too. Suddenly, my own eyes started to get wet. I turned my face into the thin pillow.

"Steve, I want to call home now so you can talk to Mom. She needs to hear from you, to know you're OK. Can we do that? It doesn't matter what time it is. Steve?"

I left my face buried in the pillow for a long time until I felt my father's weight slowly lift from the mattress.

Chapter Six

"Life is a field of unlimited possibilities."
Deepak Chopra

Snapping out of It

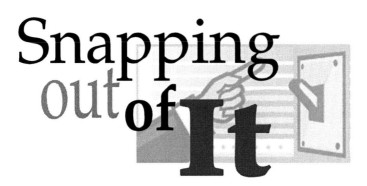

T he strangest thing that ever happened to me, the most mind-blowing *split second of my entire life*, occurred on the fourth day of captivity in that Denver basement.

The sky was overcast outside the high basement window. The blanket of cold heavy gray seemed to penetrate right into the house. I shivered when I got out of bed finally and stood up. The impression of my father's body in the mattress seemed to linger there still.

Everything was more quiet than usual. Over the past several days I had gotten used to a certain amount of activity—cooking, cleaning, people milling around. But now a thick silence lay over the basement. No food was being prepared or served. Some kind of change was in the air.

My father and Patrick's two assistants sat at the little table. They looked unsure of what they were supposed to do, where they were supposed to focus their eyes. When Patrick finally walked in, everyone stood up. They all turned to face me. Patrick had a look of calm on his face, and I could tell he wasn't preparing to confront me as aggressively as he had during the first few days of the ordeal. He gazed at me for a long time, scrutinizing me until I started to feel uncomfortable. What was he doing?

Then it happened. Patrick opened his mouth and, speaking to my father, said five one-syllable words that dramatically altered my life.

"He can go home now."

And in that split second my entire Moonie universe came crumbling to the ground. The moment before he uttered those words, I was still a True Believer, ready to fight and pray and sacrifice and purge and vomit and sell flowers on the cold streets of America for the rest of my natural life. And the moment after he uttered those words, I was . . . Steve again.

There was no space between those two realities. The shift in my mind happened someplace that was outside of time. It was not a gradual realignment of thought patterns or a slow dawning of awareness like somebody who takes a little extra time to figure out a joke. It all happened in a blazing flash.

It was true, I realized. I could go home now.

"Welcome back, Steve," said Patrick, stepping forward to shake my hand firmly. "I wish you the best of luck. You're a fine young man." Then he handed me a book. "You'll probably be interested in this now," he said. A minute later he was gone, and I never saw him again.

I had been deprogrammed.

Of course, I was extremely curious about how I had suddenly snapped out of being a Moonie. It was a disorienting experience. What were the mechanics involved? What had happened to my brain? Did other people have similar experiences? How could I assimilate what had happened to me and make sure it never happened again? What was brainwashing, and what did people mean when they used the word "deprogrammed?" Because that's what I was now and would forevermore remain: a deprogrammed human being.

There was a bustle of activity as Patrick said his good-byes to everyone else then disappeared up the stairs.

Before he left, he instructed his assistants and my father to keep talking to me, keep my mind actively thinking about the future and non-Moonie ideas. He also told them to watch their language around me, to be careful not to use any Moonie words like "love-bombing" that could potentially snap me back into my cult mindset.

Patrick didn't have to worry, though. I was the ideal client. The moment he said those five words, I was out. The change was complete. Nobody needed to keep tabs on me to make sure I didn't sneak back out to the streets and begin selling flowers again. My brain was entirely my own once again. And it all happened in the matter of a split second. Less than a split second, actually. It was instantaneous. I just snapped out of it.

Still, the strongmen kept an eye on me. The mood was lighter, and they joked around a lot, but the door at the top of the stairs was still locked. My father looked greatly relieved. We phoned home and told the rest of the family that I'd be coming home for the holidays. My mother breathed a deep sigh of relief. She had been my dad's much-needed moral and spiritual strength throughout the whole ordeal, and it had been especially hard on her to experience it all from a distance. I spent another full day in the basement before we headed to the airport the next morning. The entire time I had my head buried in the book Patrick had given me, devouring it from cover to cover before we landed back in Florida late at night on Christmas Eve.

The book is called *SNAPPING: America's Epidemic of Sudden Personality Change* by Flo Conway and Jim Siegelman. I have read it several times since then, and it has significantly deepened my understanding of what happens to people who are brainwashed into a specific way of thinking and how they can escape from it.

I learned many interesting facts in that book, including the fact that Ted Patrick himself was the person who coined the term "deprogramming." I also learned about the human brain, and how my own brain had been altered by the experience I'd been through.

Brainwashing can happen to anyone. If you have a mind, it can be altered. This is the nature of human beings. It has happened to many intelligent, educated, rich people. Even famous people have been brainwashed. It is not a phenomenon restricted to isolated discontents wandering the streets, vulnerable to these deceitful groups. What I would like to suggest here, in fact, is that it has already happened to you. Without your awareness, you've come under the influence of powerful forces that shape the way you think about the universe and your place in it, especially your financial place.

You may recall Money Secret #7 in Chapter Four, "You're on Remote Control." In that section I said, "You will never come face to face with the powerful leader who is keeping you locked in your financial situation. There is no leader. There is only a system. A concept. And this concept is controlling your every action. You have got to think your way out of this conceptual box, but unfortunately it is your very thought processes keeping you inside of it. How are you ever going to change your thoughts?"

After reading *Snapping* and researching this topic in-depth, I've come to understand that, in fact, you cannot change your deepest, most firmly entrenched thoughts. You cannot think your way out of a particular way of thinking, any more than a hamster can escape its cage by running on the wheel inside of it. You have to SNAP out of it. You have to open the cage. The remainder of this book will focus on how you can prepare your mind to snap out of its current, self-limiting patterns. First, in this chapter I will explain how the process of snapping works. Then, in Chapter Seven I will give some guidance about how to apply these principles to your own thoughts regarding success and money. In Chapter Eight, I'll outline the 30-day plan for Making the Switch to Being Rich. And finally, in the last chapter I will offer suggestions you can use to move forward toward your own personal vision of wealth.

The authors of *Snapping* went on a quest to understand what happened to growing numbers of people in America who were undergoing what they called an "epidemic" of sudden personality change. This quest led them to California's Orange County Jail where they interviewed Ted Patrick, who was imprisoned, as he had been several times, on charges of kidnapping cult members.

Their quest also took them to the laboratories and research centers of some of the world's top experts on the workings of the human mind. These scientists led them down into the rabbit hole of the brain itself where they eventually discovered the processes at work that create sudden changes in thinking.

Your Brain Lives in Dream Time

One of the scientists the authors of *Snapping* interviewed was Dr. John Layman, a professor of engineering and psychology. His launching point for exploring the way the mind works was in dreams. "When you start measuring dream lengths in relation to their content," he said, "you observe much more dream content than would seem possible in the length of time sleep is going on. The rates of dreaming don't seem to be time-bound. Another example of this phenomenon is when a person sees his whole life flash before him when he's drowning."

As Layman and other scientists delved into this and other peculiarities of the brain, they established the field of Cognitive Science, which is defined as the study of the brain's information-processing capabilities in order to understand how humans organize and make meaning of their daily bombardment of data.

As it turns out, human beings do not merely upload chunks of data (sights, sounds, words, smells, etc.), swirl them around inside their brains, and spit them back out as words or thoughts. The brain, through its intricate workings, actually transforms this information, changing it from mere signals into moving, biological patterns that are alive.

But, said Layman, this living process of transformation has its limits. The chemicals in the brain fire reactions that take place at roughly 300 feet per second, which is far slower than the 186,000 miles per second that is the speed of light and upper limit of super-fast electronic equipment. So, with something so rudimentary, how could the brain pack vast amounts of information into a tiny sliver of time, as when your entire life flashes before your eyes or you have a great epic dream that turned out to last two seconds? And how can people remember and process vast stores of information almost instantaneously, at a rate that still outperforms even the fastest supercomputer?

It turns out that time is not a factor in the internal workings of the brain. Time only becomes a factor when the workings of the brain have to be translated into the outer world. As Layman said, "We are time-bound by our ability to express." Everything your brain outputs to the world is muscular in nature. Even your words are created through the firing of your vocal chords, which are muscles. All the brain's intricate inner workings have to be put into simple sequential order to make sense in the outer world. But that is not how your brain is structured inside your head. Chronological time does not limit the inner you.

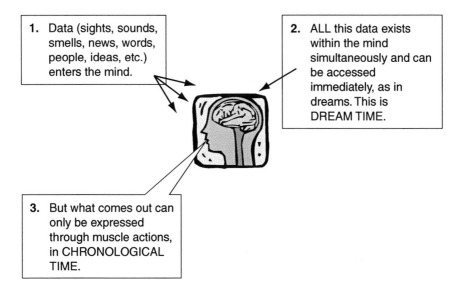

1. Data (sights, sounds, smells, news, words, people, ideas, etc.) enters the mind.

2. ALL this data exists within the mind simultaneously and can be accessed immediately, as in dreams. This is DREAM TIME.

3. But what comes out can only be expressed through muscle actions, in CHRONOLOGICAL TIME.

The inner you lives in a kind of "dream time" where everything exists simultaneously. But if you were to express yourself this way in the outer world, you would not operate very well. This is what happens to aboriginals in Australia who put themselves into their dream-time trances. They detach from the outer world, standing on one leg for hours, not even feeling it when flies crawl across their eyeballs. Layman noted that, "The brain has no moving parts and its activities need not be stretched out over time." So an aboriginal in a trance has suspended the translation of his inner world to the outer. Deep inside, you too live in a kind of dream time. Within your mind, there are an infinite variety of sequential muscular expressions you can choose to manifest in the outer world, but you consistently choose the same ones, the same patterns, over and over again. This is how you create reality.

You are familiar with how reality looks on the outside, in your daily life. But how does it look on the inside? How does your brain actually structure the vast possibilities available to it and hold particular patterns intact over time so they can be translated into the world and shared with everyone else?

The answer to that question, it turns out, may be found in the fascinating world of holograms.

Your Brain Is a Hologram

The authors of *Snapping* visited another scientist, Dr. Karl H. Pribram of Stanford University, to further their understanding of how the brain works. Dr. Pribram, an internationally acclaimed neuroscientist, explained how memory and thought patterns are not stored in separate data bits inside the brain, but rather in a vast interplay of intersecting patterns of information, very much like a hologram.

Put simply, a hologram is like a photograph, but it is three-dimensional. The image is created by a laser beam, which is split into two parts. One part illuminates the object to be holographed. The other part is a "reference beam." When those two beams recombine on a photographic plate, they form an interference pattern. Later, when that pattern is illuminated, it reconstructs the original object in 3-D. Thus, you can see an image floating "above" or "inside" your credit card or other medium.

This method can also be used to store large amounts of data because the data is stored in three dimensions rather than two.

Dr. Pribram explained that your mind works in a similar way. Consider sight, for example. Vast amounts of information enter your brain in the form of light. All of this input comes together at many levels to form interference patterns. Those patterns register beyond the retina, which acts as the photographic plate of the eye, to create 3-D images deep inside your brain. The images are then projected outward and perceived as an object in your field of vision.

You use your other senses to create your reality in a similar fashion. Your ears stereophonically reproduce the experience of sound "out there" in the world in a specific location, but actually it's just a projection of interference patterns. Your taste and smell combine in a phenomenon known as synesthesia to create interference patterns inside your mind that you experience as reality outside of you, as well.

As Dr. Pribram said, "Holograms deal with conscious awareness. When I light up a hologram, the image I see is not on the photographic film. It's somewhere beyond—it's a projection. If the brain is holographically organized, conscious experience will be similarly projected when the right input comes in."

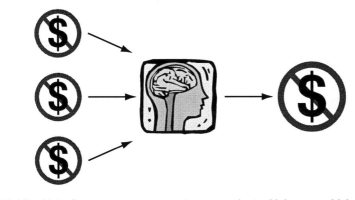

Habitual interference   *. . . project a Hologram which you perceive*
patterns in your mind . . .   *as reality "out there."*

So, rather than recording a reality that is "out there," your brain actually "projects" reality onto the world. This is the opposite of what you are used to thinking. And though it may sound like something straight out of an episode of Star Trek, it is in fact the most accurate way of explaining what is happening inside your head.

Perhaps the most fascinating detail about holograms is their ability to be completely reconstructed from only a small piece of the original photographic plate. If part or even most of the plate is destroyed, the remaining piece when illuminated will still project the entire 3-D image.

This explains the brain's ability to retrieve huge amounts of information, including the experiences of an entire lifetime, in a flash. Each piece of your brain contains the entirety of your experience. Memories and thought patterns are not stored in separate little file drawers inside your head. They're spread out. They are a product of the interference patterns inside your mind that you constantly project outward.

Have you ever had the experience of first waking up in the morning and feeling as though you had to "reconstruct" your life from the ground up? That is your mind gearing back up into its habitual interference patterns and attendant projections.

In the Moonies, I was gradually convinced through their brainwashing techniques to change the interference patterns of my mind. You too have been convinced to construct and vigilantly defend certain interference patterns within your own mind. These are the patterns that are keeping you inside the moneyless bubble.

Because this is very important, I'll repeat a core fact here: It is not just a string of thoughts inside your head that is controlling you. If that were the case, it would be simple to change. You could say to yourself, "I seem to believe money is the root of all evil; therefore, I keep money away. Starting this moment, I am going to stop thinking money is the root of all evil. Instead, I'll start to think money is good, and will therefore attract money." It does not work that way. Rather, it is your entire holographic mind, the complex mix of interference patterns that constitute your projected reality that keeps you trapped. You are your own jailer.

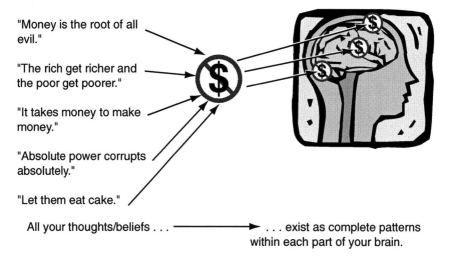

"Money is the root of all evil."

"The rich get richer and the poor get poorer."

"It takes money to make money."

"Absolute power corrupts absolutely."

"Let them eat cake."

All your thoughts/beliefs . . . ⟶ . . . exist as complete patterns within each part of your brain.

As a Moonie, I continued to experience myself as a conscious, thinking individual. It wasn't that I couldn't think. The problem was that all my thoughts flowed along the same static patterns. I could not escape my own mind's projections.

Your thoughts too are flowing inside of the same habitual patterns. It is the nature of your brain. You construct a reality to live within, and then project it out on the world. And that pattern is not located in one specific place in your physical brain. There is not one little file drawer with the thought, "Money is the root of all evil." Rather, this thought and others like it are simply snippets of the wildly swirling mass of information that makes up the entirety of your worldview. And this entirety is contained within each small piece of your mind, just like each small piece of a holographic plate contains the whole of the image.

You cannot just change a thought, or a series of thoughts, about money. You have to *Switch* the way your mind works. You have to destroy the interference patterns you currently use and tune into some new ones.

But how?

Your Brain Is a Slave to Experience

Another question remained for the authors of *Snapping*. How exactly did the mind keep reconstructing the same interference pattern over and over again? The things you focus your attention on also focuses the lens of the hologram in your mind. But why does the mind focus on the same things over and over again, seemingly without escape? Why couldn't you simply wake up one morning on a new track? This led the authors back in time to the 1950s and the work of British engineer W. Ross Ashby, the author of *Design for a Brain,* a theoretical exploration of this topic. Ashby's great insights lay in identifying the crucial need that humans have for a stream of new information and feedback from their environment.

Consider the isolation tank, for example. If you float in a temperature-controlled, soundproofed environment and cut off all sensory input, your mind quickly begins to manufacture its own experiences via visual and auditory hallucinations. Your mind cannot function normally without a constant flow of new input.

This flow, at least partially, controls who you are. We are born with a fixed number of neurons in the brain, but the synaptic connections between these billions of cells are only minimally organized. It is *through* experience that they are "hardwired" into a specific pattern. You become *through* being.

Ashby further noted that the mind organizes and attaches meaning to that endless flow of information so that you can experience growth and adapt to your environment. Ashby termed this process of organizing and adapting THE LAW OF EXPERIENCE, which states, "new information coming into a communication system [human being] tends to destroy and replace earlier information of a similar nature."

This is true for groups of people as well as for individuals, such as when people believed the Earth was flat, or that the sun, stars, and planets revolved around the Earth. Old beliefs such as these are static interference patterns in the mind, and they will stay fixed (at the time, the world did LOOK flat, and the heavens did APPEAR to revolve around the Earth) until some new experience comes along to disrupt that pattern.

Without Galileo, the world would have remained flat for millions of people. Without Ted Patrick, I would have remained a Moonie. In the same way, a "disruptor" is needed to break the pattern of poverty consciousness in your mind. You need to experience a newer, more intense and meaningful experience before you can let go of the old pattern. Without a new experience, you will not let go of the old pattern because it would feel like you were letting go of your mind itself. You would, in effect, go insane, nothing would have meaning, and you would have no reference points on which to hang the tapestry of reality.

Strangely, even experts make the mistake of thinking that the personality and belief structure of an individual is fixed, predetermined by genetic code and early upbringing. When psychologists interviewed me after my Moonie ordeal, none of them understood what Ted Patrick understood—that I could not think my way out of the group. I needed new, compelling experiences to force my mind into a new way of looking at things. The Moonies had bombarded me with a stream of persuasive new information until I eventually adapted it as my own and began focusing on that one slice of potential reality—that one holographic interference pattern. My mind, once filled with infinite potential, had been narrowed. I needed to go through the catastrophe of deprogramming to regain my freedom of mind. Simple thinking wouldn't do the trick.

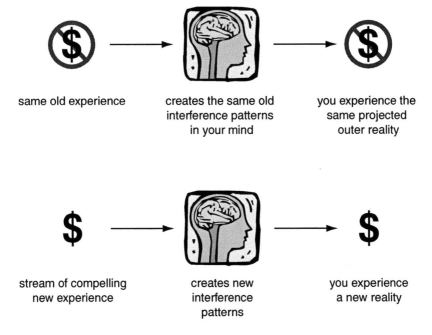

same old experience | creates the same old interference patterns in your mind | you experience the same projected outer reality

stream of compelling new experience | creates new interference patterns | you experience a new reality

You too are providing yourself with a constant stream of persuasive information and experience to maintain your current view of the world. Included in that view is the idea that seeking money is an unworthy pursuit. You value expressing yourself creatively, helping others, and making an impact on the world more highly than achieving wealth, so somehow you have the idea that those pursuits are mutually exclusive. You surround yourself with people, literature, media, and experiences that bolster that view. And that's fine. Each of us needs to live within a pattern of some kind or we would go insane. But if you are, at the same time, desperately seeking to escape this point of view, it is bound to create a huge amount of tension and unhappiness for you.

In order to change your outer reality and Make the Switch to Being Rich, you need to experience an inner meltdown, a catastrophic restructuring of your mind.

Your Brain's a Catastrophe Waiting to Happen

The authors of *Snapping* made one last stop on their journey toward understanding the workings of the brain. At the University of California, Berkeley, they spoke to an expert in the field of CATASTROPHE

THEORY, Dr. Hans Bremmermann. Catastrophe theory was first developed by French mathematician René Thom in his attempt to describe scientifically those situations in which gradually changing forces lead to so-called catastrophes, or abrupt changes. These include earthquakes, the breaking of waves, cloudbursts, and other manifestations of nature. They also include mankind's catastrophes such as stock-market crashes, riots, and, as the authors of *Snapping* were attempting to explain, sudden personality changes.

Why did the authors look to the world of mathematics for an answer to the snapping problem? One mystery that continued to puzzle them was the way in which people who snapped out of cults often did so in reaction to some trivial phrase or gesture, just as I did. When Ted Patrick looked at my father and said, "He can go home now," I was suddenly and completely changed—I was not a Moonie any more. What could account for the bizarre speed of these sudden changes in thousands of people all over the world in similar groups and thought-controlled environments? Catastrophe theory held the most promise of explaining the mechanics behind this kind of sudden shift.

In the mathematical model created by Thom, each catastrophe represents "an abrupt resolution of conflict between steadily interacting and opposing forces." In the study of earthquakes, for example, it *explains the forces behind the movement of tectonic plates and how* they move toward that point when the forces are too great and the quake finally occurs. The final half-inch move of the plates is no bigger or more important than previous ones, but it sets in motion the catastrophic event. As the authors of *Snapping* put it, "The breaking point, the final push, is wildly out of proportion to the tiny event that set it off." In other words, it's the straw that breaks the camel's back.

The deprogramming moment for a cult member, then, occurs when a critical mass of new information has streamed into the person's mind, creating tension. The new information must be in direct opposition to the old information. There eventually comes a moment when the next tiny bit of information is the straw that breaks the camel's back. For me, that straw was the phrase, "He can go home now."

René Thom created an elegant curve to graphically display the mathematics behind his theory. You can see in the drawing how change can occur gradually, along the smooth surface, or drop suddenly over the "ledge." The world of quantum mechanics describes this same ledge using another term, "discontinuity." Physicists use this word to describe what happens when an electron orbiting a nucleus instantaneously switches its orbit to a new one without ever physically existing anywhere between the two orbits.

In my case, the Moonies had strongly influenced my mind, and Ted Patrick knew that he had to stream a lot of new information into my system before I would experience a discontinuity of my own.

In your case, it's a combination of factors—family, friends, culture, media, and more—that has strongly influenced your mind, and you too need a powerful stream of new information to help you change it. Making the Switch to Being Rich, at its core, involves sending your mind a new stream of information until it reaches its own catastrophe, or discontinuity, and snaps into a new framework, a new

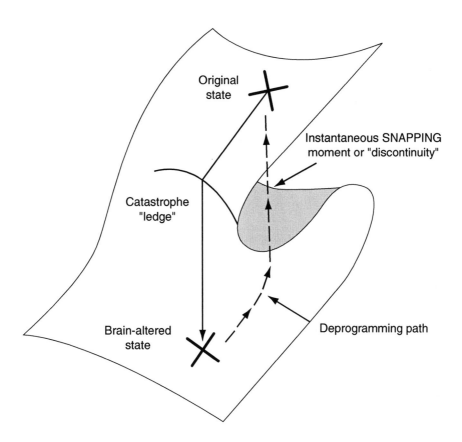

patterning of information. This new pattern (the rich you) already exists in a potential state inside the many possibilities of your mind. This is Deepak Chopra's "field of all possibilities," as explained in his book, *The Seven Spiritual Laws of Success*. This field of infinite potential is not a mystical or supernatural phenomenon. It is simply the natural ability of the mind to assimilate information, create a reality structure, and project it onto the world. This is the world that you inhabit, for better or worse, for richer or poorer.

I promised you in the introduction to this book that I would try to explain why it feels as though an invisible force is keeping money in the hands of some and out of the hands of others. I hope you are beginning to understand now that this invisible force can be found in your own mind. Specifically, it can be found in the way your mind creates and holds patterns based on the information it receives. The invisible power "out there" holding you back from achieving your goals is actually your own mind creating your particular view of reality. This ability of your mind to create reality may seem spiritual or magical, but actually it's extremely physical. Its physicality, however, lies outside of the time-bound structures of the brain. You cannot grasp it or examine it in normal, chronological terms, and so it seems to emanate from "another realm."

Look again at Thom's catastrophe curve. Each point on its supple *surface represents one possible reality structure your mind could* hold. You can change from one structure to the next gradually, or, if the new information you are receiving is powerful enough, you can fall off the "catastrophe ledge." The most extreme change, or "snap," is experienced as a "discontinuity" when your mind instantly changes from one state to a drastically different one.

Snapping into an alternate state is a matter of your mind changing its reference patterns. As we've learned, the mind operates outside the boundaries of time, as long as there is no need to express its activities through muscular action in the outer world. When you finally Make the Switch to Being Rich, the experience inside your own mind will be instantaneous, timeless, and singular.

Following the deprogramming, I spent the holidays at my parents' house in Tampa. It was strange being home. Even though my mind was once again my own, there was now a gap inside of me, an empty place six months long. Friends and family were overjoyed to see me, but at first I found it difficult to communicate. Just being me felt like putting on an act. I had to readjust to being normal. Ted Patrick had a name for this interim phase immediately after deprogramming. He called it "floating."

And that's exactly what it felt like. Even though I knew I'd never go back to the Moonies, I still thought about them a lot. I thought about the people I'd known, the people I'd sacrificed so much of my time and energy with, the people who were still there.

During this time, my body was changing rapidly. My glazed-over eyes and flabby muscles disappeared with good food and desperately needed exercise. I was getting myself back.

One of Patrick's assistants stayed with us for a week until after the New Year, "just in case." During this period, I took the opportunity to read *Snapping* again. For someone in my position, it was the most fascinating read in the world.

Here's what I learned from my reading, summed up in the following four points:

1. Your brain is not a captive of time, but the outward expression of your brain's activity, being muscular in nature, is. The timeless nature of your mind is demonstrated by its ability to create long epic dreams that last merely seconds.
2. You maintain your view of reality like a hologram within your brain, a vast swirl of information and memories that creates a specific interference pattern that is projected outward onto the world. The parts of the pattern are not found in discrete locations within the mind, but rather the entirety of the pattern is contained in all the parts.
3. In order to maintain that pattern, your brain needs a constant stream of new input. The Law of Experience states that compelling new information entering your mind will tend to destroy and replace earlier information of a similar nature.

4. After enough new, opposing information streams into your awareness, it may trigger a catastrophe which SNAPS your mind suddenly out of its old way of looking at things and into a new perspective. Your inner hologram, the way you project reality, shifts so that each part of your brain now contains the entirety of this new world view. You have "Made the Switch."

It was all slowly starting to make sense. But how could I apply this new knowledge to my own personal financial situation? And, more importantly, how can you apply it to yours?

Chapter Seven

*"I don't believe in a law to prevent a man
from getting rich."*
                    Abraham Lincoln

Destroying
the Robot
Within

So, now you know what happened to me, how the shock of de-programming wrenched me out of my limited frame of mind. But how does this apply to you? What concrete steps can you take to start the process of changing your own mind about money?

Before you can get anywhere, it is crucial to make a Switch, to snap out of your currently held view of what is right and what is wrong regarding money. Without that initial Switch, you will not be able to see your way through to another way of being. No matter how many get-rich books you read or prosperity workshops you attend, if you don't change your underlying beliefs, your investment of time and money will be wasted. You will never be rich, even if somebody were to walk up to you right this minute and hand you a million dollars. It would all be gone soon enough. The Bible itself provides wisdom on this topic: "Wealth hastily gotten will dwindle, but those who gather little by little will increase it." Proverbs 13:11

In other words, the process has to be organic and it has to start from within.

But you can't just wake up one morning and decide to snap out of your old way of thinking. You have to prepare yourself to Make the Switch, like Ted Patrick prepared me during the three days leading up to my own snapping experience. You have to gradually break down and destroy the robot within.

I hope, after reading the previous chapters, you now have a basic understanding of the dynamics involved in making an internal switch to a new frame of reference. This switch involves, among other things, a flow of compelling new information. In this chapter I am going to provide you some more of that information, putting together the final pieces of the puzzle and laying the groundwork for you to make your own Switch.

In order to accomplish this, I'll take the money secrets of the millionaire gurus and flip them completely around, revealing some opposing potential thought patterns you can use to destroy the robot within and begin gaining control of your own destiny. This is, essentially, what Ted Patrick did for me by exposing my mind to the inconsistencies and indefensible logic of the belief system I was operating under.

#	MONEY SECRETS OF THE MILLIONAIRE GURUS	OPPOSING THOUGHT PATTERN
1	YOU WANT TO BE DEPENDENT ON SOMEONE ELSE.	IT'S OK TO BE THE BOSS.
2	YOU'RE ON REMOTE CONTROL.	TAKE CONTROL.
3	WHEN YOU ARE CONFUSED, YOU ARE EASY TO MANIPULATE.	BECOME DISCIPLINED.
4	YOU DON'T TRULY TRUST YOURSELF.	TRUST YOURSELF.
5	YOU BELIEVE IN KINGS AND MOGULS.	MAKE MONEY YOUR FRIEND.
6	YOU ARE ADDICTED TO BEING GOOD.	GET REAL.
7	YOU ARE GREEDY.	MOVE BEYOND SACRIFICE.
8	YOU THINK BEING POOR MAKES YOU SPECIAL.	LIFT OTHERS UP.
9	YOU WANT OTHERS TO BE POOR WITH YOU.	
10	YOU ARE CORRUPTIBLE.	TAKE RISKS.

It's OK to Be the Boss

If you're like most people in the helping, healing, and creative professions (myself definitely included), the thought of telling people what to do, actually controlling another human being, repels you. Each individual, in your mind, is a sovereign entity, entitled to his or her own choices. Who are you to meddle in someone else's existence in such an intrusive way? Who are you to be bossing people around?

But wait a minute. If you look a little closer at yourself, you may just find that you have some boss-like characteristics that you are hiding from the rest of the world, and even from yourself. Think about it: You are, in fact, striving to make an impact on others through your chosen profession or path in life. You want to touch people in some way. You have no problem allowing others to depend on you for their education, safety, healing, insight, entertainment, or meaning. But when it comes to money, you consistently make yourself dependent on somebody else. You consistently make somebody else the boss. You refuse to make other people dependent on you for their money, even though this would create new opportunities for you, expand your horizons, and possibly make you more money. Why is that? Why are you more comfortable *with* a boss than *as* a boss?

For years, I had trouble having a housekeeper work in my home. Requesting another human being to do my laundry made me feel like a slave owner or tyrant. Who was I to boss somebody else around? When I made my own Switch, however, I started to see things differently. By providing another human being with a job, I was, perhaps, doing her a favor. I now enjoy hiring people to work for me at home and in my business. Telling other people what to do is another way of taking responsibility for them.

It is this responsibility that you are most afraid of. You're putting yourself into a submissive position so that you have an excuse not to take responsibility.

Why are you so afraid of being responsible for another human being? Because you care. You and I and all of the other caring people out there are afraid that by becoming bosses we will not care anymore. Bosses today, especially in larger corporations, have a reputation for caring more about the bottom line than about their underlings. You do not want to be uncaring; therefore, you keep yourself from being a boss. But not all bosses are bad, are they? And who better than you to be a boss? It is precisely because you do not have a burning desire to control other people that you would probably make a better boss than most.

You tell yourself you don't want to take precious moments away from your "true mission" to spend time telling other people what to do. But that's just making excuses. By putting yourself in a leadership position, you'll ultimately give yourself more freedom. By letting other people take care of some of the details for you, you'll have more time to pursue your passion. By marshalling the exponential power of other people working together, you can make an even larger positive impact in the world.

Hierarchical structures are a part of human society like roots and branches are a part of trees. Some will lead; some will follow. The choice is yours: Do you want to follow the lead of somebody whose sole purpose is profit or would you rather become a leader and offer a bigger purpose to those who follow you?

It's OK to be the boss. *Believe* me.

Listen. You already have the best intentions toward other people, right? *It is better to be a leader than it is to sit by and let others—who may even have ulterior motives—take over the daily activities and inner visions of their followers' minds and bodies.*

Many bosses, just like manipulative millionaire gurus, know that the majority of people are content to avoid responsibility and remain dependent on somebody else; that is why it is easy to control them. But if you start developing your potential to be in charge, you will make important strides toward breaking that cycle and making your own personal Switch to Being Rich. You'll find some suggestions on how to develop this potential in the next chapter.

Take Control

Now, go a little bit deeper. Take a closer look at your relationship to the bosses in your life (past or present) and focus on the underlying dynamic. What you will see, ultimately, is control. If you look closely enough at any relationship, you will find control at its root. This is normal. It is important to understand that wanting to control other people is part of being human. There is no way around it. When you are in any relationship with another person, for no matter how short a period of time or how fleeting the circumstances, you are trying to control him and he is trying to control you. If the person is a friend, you do things so she'll like you. If the person is a customer, you do things so he'll buy. If the person is an employee, you do things to ensure her compliance. If the person is a lover, you do things so he'll love you. All relationships involve control or attempts to control.

You, however, have been conditioned your entire life to fight against the concept of control. Control, you are told, is the enemy. You live in the land of the free and the home of those dedicated to fighting control. This philosophy seeps into every aspect of your life. You refuse to admit that control has its proper place in your life. So, like an adolescent, you rebel. You rebel against being controlled, complaining bitterly about your bosses. And you rebel against controlling others, claiming you do not wish to place others in submissive positions.

Make no mistake about it, though. There is no escape from control while you are still alive and relating to other people in any capacity. Control is indigenous to human beings. When you finally come to terms with this, you will be better equipped to deal with control in a calm, rational way. You can strip the emotion and rebellion from the equation and see things as they are. And at that point you will be able to deal more effectively with money and control issues arising from money.

You are faced with two choices: Either you grow up and take control of your own life, in addition to controlling parts of other peoples' lives in a mature and responsible way, or you stagnate in a role of dependence and adolescence because you refuse to take control.

This refusal may very well extend into your personal life, making it difficult to ever achieve the fully adult relationships you crave. As the authors of *The Guru Papers* suggest, "Since intimacy necessarily gives each person some power to control the other, to avoid dealing with the realities of control is to avoid growing up."

Can you see how your desire to always be the helpful, caring, non-controlling person is keeping you stuck in perpetual adolescence?

It allows others to use concepts like "duty," "karma," and "righteousness" to control you. If you snap out of that point of view, you will find a grand opportunity waiting for you. You can take responsibility in this world, right now. You can get down to the business at hand. You can grow up.

Become Disciplined

Many books have been written that feature extensive interviews with millionaires. The idea behind these books is that you, the reader, will benefit by exploring the thoughts and habits of these individuals and that perhaps you will be able to duplicate them yourself one day. This is a fine idea, but of course it will only work if you first Make the Switch to a new way of thinking. No amount of superficial imitation will change your belief system. The best of these books, such as *Think and Grow Rich,* explore deeper issues as well as external habits.

I'm a big believer in making changes that start from the inside. But there are a few outer habits explored in such books that you can begin practicing right away and that may indeed help push you toward Making a Switch of your own. One of the most important of these habits is DISCIPLINE.

Are you a "go with the flow" kind of person? Do you find yourself saying, "The Universe will provide for me?" Are you content to let much of life slide by and only take a disciplined approach to your goals when it's absolutely necessary? Guess what? This is not the ideal philosophy if you're trying to Make the Switch to Being Rich. Sure, it sounds more artistic, organic, and romantic to just go with the flow, but there will come a time in your life when a choice must be made: to go with the flow or to create a new flow entirely.

An essential ingredient of the deprogramming process is the disruption of your current thought patterns. Your current patterns cannot be disrupted until you force a new pattern into your awareness. This is where discipline comes in and this is the secret behind goal making. When you focus on a goal, the important thing is not the goal itself, which exists somewhere "out there" in the future. The important thing is the way you are exposing your mind to new patterns in the present moment, right now.

The specific goal itself, in fact, is almost arbitrary. It is infinitely more important to have a goal (some goal, any goal) than it is to have the "right" goal. Once you decide upon a goal, the trick then is to apply yourself with intensity and focus. Even if you are an extremely "go with the flow" type of person, this one new ingredient—discipline—will give you a much better chance at eventually Making the Switch to Being Rich. In fact, one of the telltale signs of an individual who has already Made the Switch is a sense of focus and purpose, which is displayed to the outside world through discipline.

You've got to make a plan.

As I mentioned earlier, everyone is susceptible to being brainwashed to one degree or another; however, because you are a caring person, your very nature makes it more likely that you will get trapped inside the moneyless bubble. Why? Because you're open. You are not a person of cold, calculating analytical thought processes. You're creative, changeable, alive, available, engaged. You allow the world and other people to have an impact on your life. The nature of your personality is susceptible to suggestion by others because you do not want to dismiss others' points of view. You want to believe that what others tell you is indeed true. You've remained an idealist longer than many others, in spite of the disheartening facts.

Perhaps it is time to get focused. It is time to choose one of the threads that has been woven into the fabric of your life and to just plain run with it. What I'm saying is that you need to choose a specific, narrow path even if this feels unnatural to you at first. You need to get "unconfused" because WHEN YOU ARE CONFUSED, YOU ARE EASY TO MANIPULATE. In an open capitalist system, the confused are taken advantage of.

You need to gain the same certainty and self-assuredness that gurus and CEOs exhibit. But how can you do that? You can start by choosing a goal or a path and then sticking to it with fierce tenacity. In my own case, I floundered for quite some time, getting fired from more than one job. Then, one day, I made the decision to apply myself 100 percent to the situation I was in at that time. I was working in a health spa, but the situation itself was not important. The act of choosing to apply myself, however, meant everything.

It's time for you to make a choice. The next chapter will give you some suggestions on what choices you can make to help nudge you toward Making the Switch.

Trust Yourself

You've been told since childhood how important it is to be a "good girl" or "good boy" so you could go to a good school, earn good grades, get into a good college, find work with a good company, follow a good career path, live in a good house in a good neighborhood, then enjoy a good retirement. The formula seems designed for your benefit. But re-read that sentence, substituting words like "obedient" or "appropriate" for the word "good," and you'll see that this insistence on goodness is a method of control. In exchange for bowing down to authority, you are promised the crumbs from the table of the banquet of capitalism. The entire process, starting from age two, molds you into a subservient role.

Now, you've grown up. You have a job and have assumed the role of caretaker, giver, or creator of some kind. You are a "good" person. But there is more to life than being good. You have to learn to trust yourself.

If you've followed all the rules and taken others' advice to heart, you may have chosen your role in life based on a fundamental lack of self-trust. Even though you have the best intentions and you do indeed help other people in meaningful ways by expressing your talents and making your mark in the world, there is still a part of you that remains unexpressed.

Being good usually means being "perceived as good" by others— parents, teachers, guardians, gatekeepers, and bosses. The act of being good carries with it a certain judgment. You are not left to your own devices to decide for yourself what is good and not good. You don't trust yourself. Instead, you look upon others as the authorities. It's practically built into your genes. You've been toeing the line all your life. What would happen if you suddenly decided to not toe the line for once, to not follow everyone else's advice, to not accept the rules at face value?

You would then find yourself out on a limb, with nobody else to trust but yourself. And this can be scary. Real scary. Making your own decisions without the guidance of someone else in a position of authority over you might result in you making mistakes. Wouldn't that be terrible?

No!

Making mistakes is exactly what you should be doing. You need to make mistakes in order to grow. Most self-made wealthy people have failed spectacularly at least once in their lives. You should be willing to do the same.

Trusting yourself, making mistakes, taking stock of the consequences, and then moving on, is crucial if you are going to position yourself to Make the Switch.

Make Money Your Friend

In your mind, you separate yourself from rich people, placing them in a different geography. They live "behind the gate" or "up on the hill," practically in another world.

You also separate yourself from money—the physical bills and coins. Money is "someplace else"—in banks, vaults, beautiful mansions, in somebody else's hands. How did it get there? Most often, it got there in exchange for something because money is, after all, a medium of exchange. And what is another word for the exchange of money for something else?

It's called selling. But you, being a good person, have dedicated your life to some purpose that is higher than the exchange of goods or services for money. You separate yourself from selling and in that way separate yourself from money itself. In his book, *The Trick to Money is Having Some,* Stuart Wilde points out that the trick to money is, in fact, having some. It can be that simple. You give somebody something and they give you money. Voilà.

But then comes the hard part. You have to *keep* the money, at least some of it, and this is where your prior conditioning may become a handicap for you. You have not been trained to keep money. You've been trained to be a "good" person who cares about people and the planet, but not money. This is what defines you. What you need to do is find someone who does not define herself in the same way and allow that person to mentor you. I'm not saying you need to be mentored by a "bad" person, but you need to be mentored by a rich person who will spend time with you to help you overcome the feeling that the wealthy are different than you. You need somebody to help you make money your friend.

At one point during my extended self-deprogramming from the moneyless bubble, I picked up another book, *Money is My Friend*, by Phil Laut. This book inspired me to take a three-week retreat with Phil in the mountains of northern California. After many days of lectures and one-on-one sessions, group processes, and meditations on the subject, I began to tune in to the feelings that I secretly harbored about money. I learned how I had subconsciously separated my sense of self-worth from money and how I had, in a sense, made money my enemy.

This was a significant realization, but it was not until later when I befriended an extremely wealthy client that I started to understand how money could actually be my friend. I discovered that even though she is worth hundreds of millions of dollars, she was exactly the same as I was in most respects, except that she did not have the separation in her mind between "worth" and "money." She could combine the two. Having money uplifted her, and she has helped many people with her wealth.

The only way to overcome your feelings of alienation from money and wealth is to delve into those feelings by getting to know the human beings behind the concepts. Every movie star is a real person. Every guru is a real person. So is every CEO, every boss, every multimillionaire, every king, and every mogul. But there is no way for you to know this, to feel it and make it viscerally real for you, until you operate on equal footing, as a friend or colleague, with one of these people. You cannot continue to be a bright-eyed groupie. You have to grow up.

This mega-wealthy friend continues to mentor me today, and I continue to learn from her. This one-on-one learning is an essential step toward Making the Switch. If you take the time, as I have, to read the extensive list of "millionaire" books out there, you'll eventually discover that they are all basically encouraging you to find a wealthy mentor. You'll find suggestions for doing just that in the next chapter.

Get Real

The world of money contains a system of immediate feedback. It is very real. When you have to deal with money in concrete terms, things suddenly come into sharp focus. Your emotions become aroused. Your thoughts are channeled directly to the matter at hand. When you are about to either give or receive a relatively large sum of money, you have an opportunity to observe the naked truth of your programming, the unconscious patterns of your mind. This can be quite a revelation. As a good, caring, helping person who usually chooses not to focus on the base reality of money, you likely spend a good percentage of your time avoiding such revelations.

Instead, you prefer to have "higher" experiences, positive interpersonal communications, and win/win encounters. You are always focused on helping and being empathetic. You are seldom concerned with getting the very best deal in any particular transaction.

Have you ever wondered why you can't just be normal and go get money? Have you secretly wished that you were someone who didn't care quite so much about everybody and everything other than yourself and your own needs? I don't blame you. You've been pressured into goodness your entire life. Your parents loved you and wanted the best for you so they sent you to school to learn how to get a good job that would help other people and benefit the community. You have been groomed to be good. What you didn't learn was how to be selfish. You were denied an understanding of the virtues of greed.

By greed, I certainly don't mean that you need to go out and steal candy from babies. Rather, I mean that you need to learn the appropriateness of your own self-interests. Most of us miss that.

It is natural to have self-interests, but by denying that natural part of your personality, you make your transactions in the financial world unnatural. Do you often feel at an unfair invisible disadvantage when it comes to transactions with people more versed in the realms of money? This is your programming at work. The long years of schooling in "goodness" have left you incapable of making a decision that is focused solely on improving your net worth.

Is it too late to change? Of course not. That is the whole premise of this book. You can change in an instant. You can Make the Switch to understanding the value of your own self-interests. By doing so, you will benefit others as well as yourself. For better or worse, you are one of the "good guys" in this world, one who cares about others and has a well-developed conscience. You've been brought up to care for and work for others, to support, entertain and uplift others. When you do eventually Make the Switch to Being Rich, all of your good qualities will not disappear—they will be magnified.

Move Beyond Sacrifice

It is not vital to other people in your life that you always make sacrifices on their behalf. It's not even important to them. What does matter is that you interact with them in a vital, meaningful way that recognizes and validates them. This point is particularly important. Trying to live up to some great ideal is not necessarily going to get you what you want in life, which is the attention and acceptance of others.

Something done willingly out of love is never a sacrifice. It is a natural, spontaneous act. Is a mother giving birth or raising a child actually sacrificing? Or is she doing what comes naturally, prodded by natural longings? Only something done in the name of an ideal, because you consider it the "right thing" despite your natural tendency to avoid it, is a sacrifice. And many of the sacrifices that you make in the name of your ideals may, in fact, not be sacrifices at all. They are attention-getting devices. You want to feel special because you have given so much, and you want others (mothers, fathers, friends, colleagues, the world-at-large) to recognize this fact.

Guess what? Everyone is special. There is no need to prove it.

When I was in the Moonies, I spent several months working with a crew that went out every morning at 6 a.m. to clean houses in Marin County, north of San Francisco. All day long I'd vacuum, dust, mop, scrub, and scour my fingers raw, all for no pay, only to support the group. At times, during those long days, I was filled with a sense of bliss so deep that I felt I was going to explode. It was a real, physical sensation in my chest. I was making the ultimate sacrifice, scrubbing toilets so that others could receive the Word of God. I had renounced the world and given up my intentions of trying to prove myself. My actions were based on an ideal.

This is the SEDUCTION OF SURRENDER. You make yourself a hero in your own mind by sacrificing for people who did not ask for that sacrifice. Joseph Campbell, a famed philosopher, said to "follow your bliss." But bliss, in the final analysis, may not be the best measure of your actions. If you are someone who is inclined to experience bliss in the act of sacrificing yourself for the sake of somebody else's happiness, it is especially important for you to learn how to *not* sacrifice yourself. Paradoxically, you need to be taught how to follow the course of action that is in your own best interests. Bliss may be something you're hiding behind in order to avoid responsibility.

Giving up can feel really good. This is the allure of sacrifice. In order to Make the Switch to Being Rich, though, you have to go beyond sacrifice. Instead of "giving up" in order to feel special, you need to learn how to "accept" in order to feel normal. This will free you up to give back to others in a healthier way, which is exactly what many rich people have dedicated themselves to doing.

Lift Others Up

One of the telltale signs of a person who has Made the Switch is a strong desire to lift up, inspire, and enrich other people. It happens every time. There is a natural tendency for people to want to bring others to their own levels, and someone who Makes the Switch to Being Rich enters a level of infinite possibilities. When you change the way your mind works, you realize that anybody else can do the same thing.

Do you sometimes see another person who you judge to be richer than you and then subconsciously wish to hold them back? Perhaps you see someone driving an expensive car and you think, "She doesn't deserve it." Or you think, "He must have done something to rip off other people in order to afford such a huge house." If you think thoughts such as these, you are feeding your mind the information it needs to stay inside the moneyless bubble.

Self-trusting people inspire self-trust in others. And truly rich people wish riches on others, even on people who seemingly already have plenty of money. One strangely effective way to open yourself to greater wealth is to be generous toward people who, in your mind, already have more than you do. It is wonderful to give to the poor, and I highly recommend it. But try giving to the rich sometime and see what happens.

Each person who moves toward success in life eventually wants to "give something back" to those who have helped her along the way. Develop your own "giving back" mentality now, even before you begin to think of yourself as rich, and this will help you Make the Switch that much faster. In the next chapter I'll offer some ideas to help you accomplish this.

Take Risks

If everything's not on the line, you won't be sufficiently motivated to Make the Switch. When I found myself in that dark Denver basement, Ted Patrick didn't say to me, "If we can't come to an agreement, you can just go back to the Moonies and continue with your chosen life." It was the end of the line. I was in the basement for as long as it was going to take. There was no place else to go, no other options available.

In order to create that kind of do-or-die mentality for yourself, you need to be willing to take some risks. You have to be willing to radically change your old way of thinking, and the way you do this is by creating a completely new set of rules for your mind to operate under. I'm not saying you need to lock yourself in a basement and talk yourself out of your poverty mentality. Rather, you've got to bombard your mind with a large amount of new information. And you've got to make it clear to your mind that there is no going back.

In the real world of money, this means you have to find something that you believe in, whether it's a new business, a new job, a new product, or a new idea, and then take risks in order to make it happen. I'm not talking about risking your life or the lives of your children. I'm not talking about risking your health. But you have to be willing to risk your self-image. You have to be willing to risk change.

One of the biggest issues that may hold you back as you strive to Make the Switch is your fear of becoming corrupt. You may believe that by focusing on money you will be "selling out." You think you will be putting yourself at risk for corruption because money and wealth bring power, and, as we all know, absolute power corrupts absolutely. You, as a good, caring individual, will avoid that possibility at all costs.

The way you overcome this fear is by first admitting that it is real. You need to admit that you can in fact become corrupted because you are human. You need to risk the chance of making mistakes. Risk the possibility of becoming materialistic. It has happened to people before and it will happen again, perhaps even to you. But you must move forward through that fear. You need to trust yourself.

It is indeed possible that you could be consumed by materialism at some point along your journey. That shiny new car might be just too tempting. That bigger house might suddenly make sense. You might find yourself obsessing over that watch, that television, those fine shoes. But if you do not risk feeling this materialism, you will never get the chance to move through it and go beyond it.

You are already a person of purpose, someone who cares about people and the planet. That is why you're reading this book. Consider yourself lucky because you've already found what many others, rich and poor, still yearn for—a moral center that goes beyond politics, religion, or even the laws of the land. It is the essence of who you are. You can indeed be knocked out of orbit from your moral center if you become too enmeshed in material pursuits. But then you can right yourself. You can enlist your support network of friends, family, and colleagues to get yourself back on course. As long as you keep your mind open, you can find your center again, realign yourself with your purpose, and move on.

The next chapter consists of a 30-day program full of calculated risks that will help you Make the Switch to Being Rich.

Are you ready?

*"Abundance is not something you acquire. It
is something you tune into."*
Wayne Dyer

Making the
Switch
to Being
Rich

O K, here you are. You've prepared your mind by exposing it to a constant stream of new information throughout the previous chapters. You're receptive to entering an entirely new frame of mind. You're ready. It's time, finally, to get deprogrammed from your financially limited point of view. But how, exactly, are you supposed to do that? Does it just happen by itself now that you understand the dynamics of what's happening in your brain? Can you simply think your way out of the moneyless bubble?

The answer to that question, as we've seen, is "no." You cannot think your way out. You have to be forcibly removed. You have to kidnap your brain. You have to lock it in a dark Denver basement, grasp it by the shoulders, sit it down, and put it through a process it will never forget. In order for my deprogramming to be effective, Ted Patrick followed certain procedures that he'd honed through a lot of experience. You now need to follow certain procedures of your own if you are to Make the Switch. They will not be the exact procedures that Patrick used for obvious reasons, but the plan laid out in this chapter is analogous to my deprogramming experience.

Many of the suggestions on the following pages involve taking real action in the real world. The reason for this is clear. If you do not force your mind into experiencing new and compelling input, you will not be able to change it. Being kidnapped and deprogrammed is an intense, overwhelming experience. That's what this chapter will attempt to simulate for you.

You never know when or where the Switch may occur for you. I Made the Switch to Being Rich one frigid February weekend in the suburbs north of Dallas. I was there teaching a workshop to massage therapy students. The company that sponsored me and advertised the workshops had given me a mandate: I was to sell $1,000 worth of their products to the students. In turn, I would receive a commission for the sales.

I hated selling. I hated everything about it. I wanted to be a teacher, a therapist, a healer. I wanted to save the world one person at a time. I did not want to become a "used car salesman." But I would force myself, each weekend, to stand in front of the students in the workshops I taught in cities across the country, and I'd try to sell them products.

I was very bad at selling. I never reached my $1,000 goal. I'd sell $300 worth of stuff some weekends. Sometimes, I'd sell less. Once, I made it all the way to $997, but it felt as though some invisible barrier was holding me back. I was stuck inside the moneyless bubble. I could not go past $1,000, even with twenty or thirty people in the class.

Then it happened. I stood up in front of a small class of only nine students in Dallas preparing to launch into my sales pitch yet one more time, when suddenly I froze. I could not stand the thought of another forced, unnatural attempt at being something that I was not. Something inside me *snapped,* and instead of my normal pitch, I blurted out an impassioned speech that surprised me probably more than it did the students. "I'm supposed to sell you this stuff," I said. "The company I work with wants me to sell you $1,000 worth of products this weekend, but I am tired of trying to sell. All I want to do is teach you. I want to give you techniques that will earn you more money and help you make your clients feel better. If you want any of the stuff in this room, just ask me. It's all for sale. But I am not going to give you a sales pitch and try to get you to buy it. That's not why I'm here. What I care about is *you.*"

The students blinked at me, like children blink at adults who clearly and forcefully lay down the ground rules. That weekend I sold $9,000 worth of products.

The moment I spoke those words to the students, I finally became honest. I finally spoke from a place of integrity and wholeness while at the same time clearly stating that I was available to receive money. I Made the Switch. Now, I personally earn $10,000 a weekend for teaching similar workshops. I sell thousands of dollars worth of products every time. It feels easy.

Perhaps your goals are much higher than an income of $10,000 per weekend. I personally consider this a steppingstone on the way to earning much more. Once your mind has been freed, you'll be able to see the tremendous possibilities all around you. Perhaps you know that if you could only Make the Switch, you could earn millions. Or perhaps you would be happy with much less. The point is to fundamentally change the way your mind works so you can operate from a position of integrity and self-confidence while asking for and accepting much more money in your life. When you achieve this, you will be naturally enthusiastic and people will respond positively to you. You will no longer build a barrier that prevents other people from giving to you. People can feel it when you're inside the bubble. They don't know exactly why, but they know they are not supposed to give you their hard-earned cash. Break free, and the money starts to flow.

It is important to note that my Switch did not occur in a vacuum. I had been preparing myself for a long time. I went on that three-week retreat with Phil Laut, read book after book about money, attended multiple seminars, took speaking and acting classes to improve my presentation, and even locked myself in a hotel room one weekend and listened to endless tapes about financial freedom. Most important of all, I put myself out in front of other people and declared that I wanted to move to a new level. I MADE MYSELF AVAILABLE. By following the steps in this chapter, you will be making yourself available, too. These are the steps I actually followed myself, and I feel confident suggesting them to you. I'd never ask you to do something I wasn't willing to do or that I didn't find useful.

What if you decide not to follow these steps? What if you're afraid of all this action? What if you don't think you can do it? That's OK. You are living your life as best you know how, so far. There is much rejoicing in simplicity, in doing your part, in being a good person. Just going to work in the morning and pitching in like everyone else can be vastly reassuring and a spiritual experience in its own right. But if you feel an incredible tension between the person you are now and the person you want to become, so much so that you are not comfortable leading the life you are presently leading, then you owe it to yourself to act and follow the steps outlined below.

And, as they say, it doesn't hurt to try. At the very least, this program will open your mind to unexplored possibilities. If you make an honest attempt at it, I will strive to support you in your efforts. Visit www.makingtheswitchtobeingrich.com for further information and other resources.

30-Day Making the Switch Program

You don't need to perform the following steps in chronological order. You can accomplish some in a single day; others should be focused on throughout the 30-day period. The program is supposed to be an organic ongoing process. It does not lead up to one particular moment on day 30 when a sudden revelation will occur, so do not focus too much on the future. Just apply yourself each day to the tasks at hand and keep persevering. The Switch could take place for you at any time during the program, or even after you've completed it. These 30 days could be the first steps on a longer journey. It took me months of dedicated effort before I experienced my own Switch, but mine occurred through a haphazard, unfocused approach. Following all of the steps below in the concentrated space of 30 days will jumpstart your mind into a new frame of reference and give you the best chance at Making the Switch sometime in your near future. I wish you the best of luck!

Step One: Kidnap Your Brain

All the best intentions in the world will not budge your financial situation even one penny's worth. In order to change on a fundamental level, you've got to be forced into it. You need to take yourself out of your habitual patterns and, for the next 30 days, enter a new world filled with unfamiliar influences. Since you will not be physically kidnapped like I was and no strongmen will be standing by to keep you locked up, you need to be forced voluntarily.

You have to be your own enforcer. To accomplish this, I suggest you prepare a little ritual for yourself at the beginning of the first day. This does not have to be exotic or esoteric. It is enough to simply sit down for ten minutes and make yourself consciously aware of the new venture you're agreeing to embark upon. You might choose to put this into writing. Using your own words, compose a letter of agreement with yourself. Or, if you prefer, use the letter below, rewriting it yourself on the computer or by hand in order to lodge it in your subconscious and make it your own. Fill in the blanks, sign it, and put it someplace readily available.

Then, for 30 days in a row, become a prisoner of your own intentions. Make those intentions effective by bringing yourself back to your purpose again and again. Each morning, take a moment to look at this agreement once more. Whenever you feel uninspired or discouraged, remind yourself of your original goal, which is to improve your circumstances and free yourself up in order to help exponentially more people and have a much bigger positive impact on the world.

"I, _____ , agree to spend the next 30 days actively focused on changing the habitual patterns of my mind. I understand that I reinforce these habitual patterns on a daily basis, minute by minute, and it will take a concerted effort on my behalf to overcome this programming.

I am steadfast and unstoppable in my desire to Make the Switch to Being Rich, because this will free me to pursue my larger vision, expand my ability to help others, and lead a more meaningful life.

When I experience self-doubt during these 30 days, I will replace it with self-trust.

When I experience uncertainty, I will replace it with self-confidence.

When I experience judgment of myself or others, I will replace it with acceptance.

For these 30 days, I will closely watch my words and my thoughts. Each time I become aware of one of my old habitual patterns, I will stop and open myself to new possibilities. The experiences I have during this period will stretch me beyond my normal capacities, but I will not waver. I will take bold action, and through these actions I will make myself available for change."

Signed _____

Date _____

Step Two: Lock Your Brain in the Basement

You have to make the experience of these 30 days physically real. You have to confine your mind and focus yourself, the same way I was forced to focus when I was held prisoner in a basement. In order to do this, it will help to follow a few basic guidelines:

- Set a schedule. Get your mind accustomed to new activities and experiences by forcing yourself to engage in them at specific times on specific days. If you don't set a schedule, your mind will drift and you will procrastinate until the 30 days are over.

■ Eat well. A healthy, balanced diet will give your mind the fuel it needs to absorb the new experiences it will encounter during these 30 days. If you are stuck in some unhealthy eating patterns, as I was in the Moonies, this is a good time to break them, as it will strengthen your mind and body so you can more readily make the changes you seek.

■ Exercise. If you don't normally exercise, this is an excellent time to start. Your physical stamina and overall health are important in order to keep up a positive attitude when faced with new challenges. If you already exercise, continue to do so throughout this program. If you are not currently exercising, walking for just half an hour every other day is enough. It is important to do something. Get yourself moving.

■ Mix up your routine. Do things differently than you normally do, even little things. Watch less TV or different shows. Take a different route when you drive to work. Disrupt the patterns your mind uses every day to prepare it for change.

■ Recommit to the program each day. Spend five minutes focusing on your intentions each morning.

Step Three: Watch Your Language

During the program, record your experiences in a Making the Switch Journal you've designated just for this purpose. Each day, write down the phrases or words that pop into your head or out of your mouth regarding money. Try to catch yourself each time. It may not be easy at first, but will become easier with practice. Note what triggered the thought or what happened immediately prior to having the thought. Observe how you feel when you utter phrases like "money is the root of all evil" or "the rich get richer, and the poor get poorer." Day by day, become more aware of your habitual thought patterns about money. The simple act of placing awareness on these patterns will help you begin to dissolve them. Deprogramming, as Ted Patrick said, is basically just sitting people down and asking them challenging questions. You too have to challenge your pre-programmed way of thinking. Do this on a daily basis as often as possible, and keep track of it by writing it down. The following are some sample Making the Switch Journal entries.

Making the Switch Journal

December 4, 9 p.m.: I spent the afternoon window-shopping with Mother. When we went into the Cole Haan store, I began fantasizing as usual about all the beautiful things in there I wanted to buy. I picked up a pair of shoes and Mother said, "Whew, look at that price. What do you think, money grows on trees?" That's when it struck me . . . I've used the exact same phrase over and over again myself. Do I believe money grows on trees? Of course not. But I guess I've come to believe, somehow, that it does for certain people: the people who can afford the shoes I want! I've been subconsciously putting myself in that class of people who cannot afford certain things. Even if I had the money, I'd look at buying shoes like this as a waste because I've been programmed to think this way.

December 5, 8 a.m.: Watched the news this morning. Saw Prince Charles and one of his cockamamie plans to benefit mankind and, as I usually do, I thought to myself, "Rich bastard! What does he know about mankind?" There I go again, thinking that the rich live on some other planet. I'm believing in Kings and Moguls, like they're different than me. Why can't I just accept the possibility that he's a real human trying to do something good?

Step Four: Discipline Yourself

You've heard the recommendation before about paying yourself first and you've thought it was a good idea. Now it's time to actually do it. One day early in the program, pay a visit to your local bank. Open a new savings or investment account. Put some money in the account, even if it's a very small amount. Then, for every dollar you earn during the 30 days, deposit a dime in that account. If it's possible, deposit more. This money is now saved and it has one purpose: growth. If you already have a savings account, start depositing 10 percent of your income into it. Ideally, you will make these deposits automatic by signing up for a plan that deducts them from your paycheck or from your checking account. If you have no checking account, walk physically to the bank and give the cash to the teller.

The only way to have money is to keep some. Most people fail to make that simple connection. If you don't have any income during the 30 days, take some other money you already have and devote it to savings instead of spending. If you do not have any money or any income, ask somebody if you can borrow it. Then save it. Pay the person back as soon as possible with money you earn. It does not take much to open a savings or investment account, but the benefit to your subconscious mind will be tremendous.

You've also heard the recommendation to live within your means. This is another very good idea. For the duration of the 30 days, practice it religiously. If a purchase is going to put you into debt, do not make the purchase.

You've surely seen the graphs and charts explaining how money grows more the longer you have it. Each day that you continue to postpone starting your 10 percent savings account, and each day that you spend money you do not actually have, you are wasting an exponentially larger amount of money that you could have in the future. Your actions make an impact. If your mind is forced into acknowledging that your actions are inevitably leading you toward being rich, the impact of this knowledge will help you to Make the Switch that much faster.

Take a look at The Power of Compound Interest graph. This shows that earning just 5 percent interest on $100 a month in savings will net you nearly $145,000 after 40 years. Without the interest, your savings would have amounted to only $48,000. This is another good reason to start your savings account ASAP. By letting your money work for you, instead of working for money, you end up with much more money than you could have otherwise.

The Power of Compound Interest

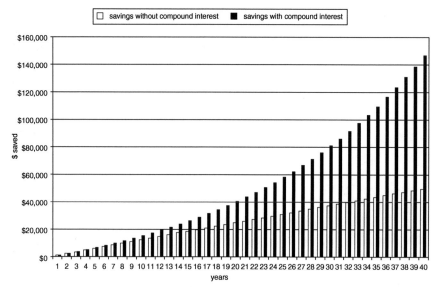

□ savings without compound interest   ■ savings with compound interest

Here's another quick, concrete way to discipline yourself regarding money. Take the next $100 bill that comes into your possession, fold it into quarters, and slip it into a back pocket of your wallet or purse. Then leave it there. That's it. It's meant to stay there. Under normal circumstances, you shouldn't spend it on anything, but it can come in handy in an absolute emergency. This bill will be a physical reminder that you are a person who has money. You'd be amazed at the number of people who have a hard time hanging on to even one single bill like this. Periodically, when you're alone, take it out and look at it. Remind yourself: The trick to money is having some. You have some.

Step Five: Stop Complaining

In your Making the Switch Journal, note down all the times you find yourself complaining about things. When you complain, you are basically admitting that somebody or something has power over you. Often the person you complain about the most is your boss. The thing you complain about most is your job. Or you may complain about the "economy" or "politics" or any other number of external forces creating your financial situation.

The point of this exercise is not to prove that your job, or boss, or whatever doesn't deserve to be complained about. The point is, during the 30-day program, to take complete responsibility for your thoughts and words.

Watch your mind. See how, through complaining, you put yourself in a lower position in relation to others, a place without power, a place where all you can do is gripe. Each time a complaint arises, whether it is legitimate or not, write it down. Examine it objectively. Separate it from yourself and don't buy into it. For these 30 days, take the opportunity to explore what it's like not to blame. As you do this consistently, you'll find that your mind gradually shifts toward thoughts and feelings of self-reliance rather than dependence. This, in turn, will move you toward Making the Switch.

Step Six: Choose a New Leader

Right now there is a good chance that you subconsciously allow some authority figure to influence your financial life. A boss. A supervisor. A CEO. Even a distant figure such as a political leader or financial celebrity like Charles Schwab.

In order to move closer to Making the Switch, you need to choose another authority figure. In the same way that Ted Patrick told me he was taking the new "alpha male" role in my life by using the pushup contest and other techniques, you need to push out the old authority figure to make room for the new one. You need to consciously choose a new role model.

The official name for this new role model of yours is "mentor." You need to choose your financial mentor wisely. Make sure it is somebody who thinks of you as more than an employee, more than who you've always been in the past. It should be a person who thinks you have great potential, and somebody who is willing to work with you and nurture you on the way to greater things. Ask this person formally to be your mentor.

I know it's scary to ask somebody else to mentor you. It may feel like an imposition, but then again, it may feel like a compliment to that person. You do not have to ask for a huge amount of his or her time. An occasional meeting is enough to get you thinking in new ways. Simply having somebody you respect say she believes in your potential for Making the Switch is extremely important.

Your mentor does not have to be a multimillionaire or businessperson. Rather, she should be somebody you admire for living a life of *purpose and choice, someone who is not stuck inside the money-less bubble.* Her line of work is not important and does not need to reflect your own career choices. Your mentor could conceivably be somebody in your family or within your close circle of friends, but often these people already have preconceived notions of your potential and could end up holding you back despite their best intentions. Take a risk and ask somebody who you are afraid might say no. If your first choice is too busy or not interested, ask somebody else. Then, during these 30 days, sit down at least one time for a chat. Ask your mentor how she envisions you moving toward your potential for greater abundance. You may be surprised at what you learn.

Step Seven: Make a Choice

All people who make a move toward greater goals in their lives have one thing in common: They chose to make that move. They choose to change their lives. You cannot change the things about yourself you want to change unless you first choose to do so. And if you do not choose, somebody else will choose for you. There are plenty of people out there willing to step in and tell you the best course of action. Usually, those people have their own best interests in mind, not yours.

What specific choices can you make that will head you off in the right direction? Only you can answer this question. In order to determine the best choices to make, first take an inventory of where you find yourself right now. Using your journal, write down the major choices you have available regarding your finances and your direction in life. You probably mull these issues over on a daily basis, but it helps to clarify and quantify your options.

Could you conceivably switch jobs within the same industry? Could you move to another department in your present company? Could you start your own business? Could you move to another city and start out on a new path? Could you quit your present career track and look for something entirely new?

You have multiple choices available to you at any given moment. Some seem much more realistic than others, but the secret is to choose. Simply make a choice. The specific content of the choice is not as important as the act of choosing itself.

In order for this choice to have a meaningful impact on your life, it should be somewhat challenging—even a little scary. It should exhibit self-trust and self-confidence. It is perfectly fine for this choice to be in your own self-interest. You do not have to prove yourself to be "good" by making the "right" choice.

In my own case, perhaps the most important career choice I made was to simply stay in my present position, working as a massage therapist for $15 an hour at a spa in Miami. Why was this a scary choice for me personally? Because, up until that point, I had always chosen to move on when any particular position became too challenging or too boring. I quit or was fired from job after job. At one point, I finally decided that I needed to prove to myself that I was capable of making a commitment.

Step Eight: Make a Commitment

Once you've chosen a specific course to follow during this 30-day period, resolve to stick to it with fierce tenacity. If your choice is to stay in your present situation, even if it involves flipping burgers or sweeping floors, do something *extraordinary* in that situation. Take full responsibility for your actions and for the relationships you form while performing these actions. Treat everyone you come into contact with, from the doorman to the CEO, with the utmost respect. Know that your outer experience is a reflection of the thoughts you project onto your situation. As you'll remember from the discussion in Chapter Six, your brain uses a constant stream of feedback to help it alter and shape your reality. If you begin giving yourself new feedback, you will begin to perceive reality in a slightly new way. Do this with increasing frequency during the 30 days. Keep asking yourself how you would act if you had already Made the Switch. How would you talk to other people? How would you be spending your time? Commit yourself fully to acting, talking, and behaving this way. Fulfill all your tasks impeccably, going beyond the call of duty. Invest yourself fully in each activity. Speak with integrity, as if you were being held to a higher standard than you are used to. You are, in fact, being held to a higher standard, because you are creating it for yourself.

I realize that following this advice will create a somewhat unreal situation because you are not in the perfect situation already. You are not completely satisfied. You are not really 100 percent convinced that this choice you've made will lead you precisely where you want to go. You are not supremely self-confident. So, am I asking you to fake it?

I don't consider it fake for you to act in your own best interests and make your own decisions. I don't consider it fake for you to decide, regardless of what happens, to be in control of your own mind for 30 straight days.

The point is, for this finite time period, to not let some authority "out there" tell you it's impossible to raise yourself to another level or that it's impossible to change your mind about what you deserve. By redirecting the responsibility for your own state of mind back onto yourself, you are simply taking control back from those people you've given it to subconsciously.

Make a commitment. Follow that one choice you've made, throwing yourself into it with your body and soul, giving 100 percent to the endeavor. For 30 days, do not hold anything back, even if you are working for somebody else during this period. Making a choice and committing yourself to following it will lead you in the right direction, even if you are not precisely sure where you are ultimately headed.

Step Nine: Incorporate Yourself

In the success workshops I teach for massage and spa professionals, I always recommend that my students create a corporation. Creating a corporation is not a big deal. Just search for the word "incorporate" on the Internet, and you'll find a number of options. The cost is relatively reasonable, usually just $200 in the U.S. or $500 in Canada. In addition, it may cost you a few hundred dollars more each year for accounting services on a corporation. But the tax advantages you gain from incorporating can more than make up for this expense in just one year. Every penny you spend to support your business can be written off as an expense.

Beyond the monetary advantages of incorporating, there are still more important psychological advantages. The act of incorporating will force your mind to come up with ways to pour money into this new business entity. Any money you make that does not come directly from an employer's pre-taxed paycheck can be effectively channeled through your corporation. This fact will inspire you to start seeking alternative income streams. It will also force your mind to realize not all corporations are evil. Your corporation will certainly not be evil, right?

I'm fully aware of the potential pitfalls of the modern corporation, how they are potentially destructive to the environment and to mankind. I am not suggesting that you structure a corporation to conceal some wicked activities of your own. I am suggesting that the business structure of the corporation has certain advantages and, when used wisely, can actually help people. More specifically, it can help you help people by making it more profitable for you to pursue your dreams.

You probably think that rich people and rich companies have corporations. You did not think of yourself as having a corporation. That can be changed with a single phone call or by filling out a single form on the Internet. Although this simple action in itself will not make you rich, it will help push your mind toward Making the Switch.

Step Ten: Make One Thing

I changed my life one day when I took eight blank pieces of paper, turned them sideways, folded them in half and stapled them together. On those pages I wrote several simple one-page stories. Then I gave it a title, *Getting the Most Out of Massage*. On the front cover, I put a price: $4.95. This was my first book.

I did not sell many copies. Hardly any, in fact. But more important than selling my book was the fact that I had actually *made* something. I had created an object people could hold in their hands and potentially find value in. I received a lot of positive feedback from this little endeavor and a bit of money, too. It was a small, but crucial first step on my own path toward Making the Switch.

You too need to make something or provide a service that will be of value to another person. It has to be something that somebody will be willing to buy. This simple step will give your mind the message that you can create income through the creative process, not just through working for somebody else. Taking this step will awaken your entrepreneurial spirit.

The object you create or service you provide should be aimed more toward making people want to purchase it than toward showing off your incredible talents. In other words, you should be thinking about the potential user of the object more than yourself. This makes it less of an artistic expression and more of a commodity. Artistic expression is fine. I practice artistic expression myself through fiction writing and other outlets. But what you're striving to create here is a commodity. Perhaps you react against the term "commodity" because it seems too commercial, superficial, and only about money. Precisely!

The types of objects you could create are endless, but it helps if they are easily reproducible, such as: booklets, e-books, videos, instructional material, souvenirs, keepsakes, postcards, novelty items, promotional items, etc.

You do not need to spend thousands of dollars and hire a patent attorney to create a saleable object. My own book of eight folded pages was complex enough, but your idea can be even simpler. In fact, the simpler the better.

Step Eleven: Sell One Thing

The next crucial step after you've made one thing is to sell one thing. Believe me, I know how intimidating selling can be. Selling turned me off more than anything else during my own journey to increased prosperity. In fact, I dedicated the first 30 years of my life to not selling. I was an anti-selling crusader. I even hated to buy things, especially if it involved haggling of any kind. I wanted to touch and heal, and teach and connect. Selling, it seemed to me, was just the opposite.

But, as you'll recall, selling was the key ingredient in my own Switch. It was by forcing myself to sell something that my own mind finally snapped, and I was able to see things in a new light. You too should be on the lookout for the one thing during these 30 days that seems most difficult or anti-you. If it is selling, then jump in! Go crazy with your selling ideas. Make them fun and off the wall. I took my booklet to a local health food store and actually sold some there on consignment, which means I made no money until the store actually sold some copies. If you want to really push yourself, you can try selling door to door. Try to avoid selling to friends and family, who may offer you your first sale out of pity or love more than the desire to actually buy what you're offering.

A couple caveats: You will probably not set off any legal alarms if you sell one simple, inexpensive item to one other person. If you expand your sales activities, however, you should be aware of local rules and regulations. You may, for example, need a resale license from your city, county, or state in order to sell things legally. If you're thinking of making and selling products that people will eat, apply to their bodies, or use to improve their health and well-being, you may need to go through the FDA or other regulatory agency. Always check to make sure you're doing things legally before you make a big investment of your time or money.

Step Twelve: Distribute One Thing

Perhaps even more important than selling one thing that you have made is selling something that somebody else has made. Why? Because this separates your own personal creative process from the act of receiving money. It pinpoints and isolates your "receiving muscle."

Some of the wealthiest individuals in the world have made their fortunes simply by distributing things. It's a strange but simple idea: Buy something for a certain amount of money, and then sell it for more. This simple idea may turn you off. It may feel like a waste of time. This is not your mission, right? You're here to help. You're here to make a difference. How is simply distributing something going to help you achieve your greater purpose in life?

No matter what it is you do, if you're going to be successful enough at it to really make a difference, you are going to need to learn how to "get in the way of the money" that is constantly flowing between people all around the world. You're going to have to get used to that feeling, and the most direct way to experience it is to simply distribute one thing.

Many unique distribution models exist that offer people the opportunity to enjoy the advantages of becoming a "distributor" without going through all the costs of building infrastructure and employing staff. In fact, thousands of people have in effect become one-person distribution companies on their own, marketing and selling from one to several hundred products. These items are offered by manufacturers who wish to engage the power of word-of-mouth or "network marketing" to get their products into the hands of as many people as possible.

For better or for worse, there is a whole lot of money flowing between people every day all around the globe. What your intention should be regarding step number twelve is to "get in the way of the money." When people channel their money through you, they are channeling their work, their hopes, their needs, their desires, their life energy. The point is to act as a conduit for this energy, and in order to do that you have to make yourself available. That is the key— making yourself available.

Of course, you're not going to be inspired about going out and selling something that you do not care about. It is helpful if the item you buy and sell aligns with your purpose. For example, in my workshops I buy and sell products that my colleagues can use to help their clients and increase their profits. I buy and sell because I care. You can do the same.

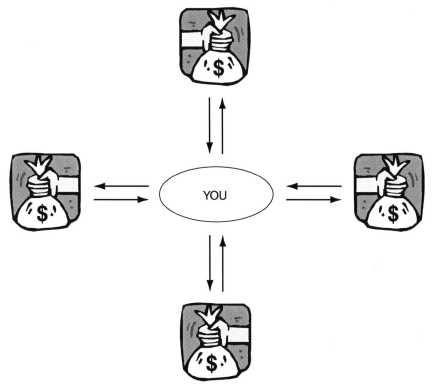

"Getting in the way" of the flow of money

Step Thirteen: Thank People for the Money

I've spent my career working as a massage therapist in the health spa industry. If there is an entire group of people who are almost all inside the moneyless bubble, it's massage therapists. We want to help people and heal them. We want to ease their aching muscles and soothe their unquiet souls. We want meaningful interactions with our clients. We do not, for the most part, want to focus on the monetary aspects of our jobs. We feel it's OK to get paid by a big "evil" spa or other corporation, but taking money from another human being is scary.

You might find yourself in the same situation. The thought of taking other people's hard-earned cash makes you feel queasy. You feel you're making it harder for them to survive. You believe, when it's time to accept their money, you're taking something away from them.

When it comes time for massage therapists to accept payment from their clients, many will say, "Please leave a donation on the table on the way out." They turn their heads and look away when it is time to receive money. They do not even want to touch the stuff.

Money is physical. And, because it is a medium of exchange that represents the time and efforts of people, it also embodies an energy all its own. Have you ever seen a huge pile of cash or big lumps of gold? You can feel the potential energy within it ready to unleash a storm of activity, almost like uranium atoms in a bomb. You, as somebody inside the moneyless bubble, are protecting yourself from that energy. You are shielding yourself from the forces released when money changes hands.

When I teach my workshops, I sometimes have participants do an exercise I call, "Thank you for the money." They pair off, then each takes out a bill, either $5, $10, $20, $50, or $100, and hands the bill to his or her partner. Each time, the receiving partner looks the other in the eyes and says, "Thank you for the money." This is only partly tongue-in-cheek. It often creates an emotional response all out of proportion to the exercise itself. This response is greatly magnified *if the people give the money to their partners for real. They are told* to take out a bill that they are actually willing to give up in that moment and that will not burden them or their families financially. Then, when they exchange the money, something powerful often happens.

This is what I am suggesting you do, as well. If, during the 30 days, you receive money from somebody, stop and take a moment to acknowledge it. Thank them for the money. You might be surprised to find that people want to be thanked. They want to be recognized for having made the choice to support you.

If you are not receiving money directly from somebody during the 30 days, create a little exercise to simulate the situation. Find a willing partner, then practice handing a bill back and forth. If you want to take this experience a step further and your partner is willing, ask her to choose a bill she is willing to sacrifice and to give it to you for real. Accept the money into your hands. Hold it there. Then look into her eyes. Thank her deeply and sincerely. She has just symbolically given part of her time and efforts—life energy—to you. If you learn how to receive this energy with respect, gratitude, and integrity, you will take another step toward Making the Switch.

Step Fourteen: Invest in Something

You may have the impression that rich people invest in the stock market. You may have tried investing yourself. Did you become rich? If not, what held you back? Did you do something wrong?

Whether you consider yourself an investor or not, you may fail to realize what investing actually is. Most people inside the moneyless bubble think that investing is an action, that it requires doing something. Actually, investing requires not doing something. It requires that you do not spend the money. And it requires that you do not work to increase the amount of money. It requires that you sit back, do nothing, and let the money do the work for you.

This is harder than it sounds. If you are a "good" person whose sense of self-worth is tied to how much you contribute to the world, and you use your income as a barometer that tells you how effective you are at playing your part, you may be subconsciously holding your money back from doing the work it could do. If you let it, your money, in effect, could outshine you and make you superfluous. So, you choose the wrong stocks. Or you choose the right stock but buy in at the wrong time. Or you sell at the wrong time. You always manage to find some way for the investment not to work out the way you had hoped.

Investing, of course, is not confined to the stock market. This dynamic applies to investing in anything, from real estate to antiques to foreign currencies to baseball cards. If you believe where you get your income at least partially reflects who you are, you will not let your money work for you. Somehow, your investment will not pan out. You won't benefit by it. Other, "rich" people's investments will be lucrative, but not yours. How can you change this?

One of the key insights you gain when you Make the Switch is this: You are already worthy. You are already who you are. You already deserve to have money come to you. There is no need to prove it. When Ted Patrick said, "He can go home now," I suddenly and paradoxically "became" the person I already was. I was Steve again. I didn't have to prove it to myself or anybody else. In fact, the thought of having to prove it is laughable, right? The thought of you having to prove your worth by earning money in a certain way is equally laughable.

You may be allowing yourself to receive money only through those channels that prove you are a good, worthy, qualified, special individual. Think back to the millionaire gurus' money secret #8: "You think being poor makes you special." This is another way of saying that you are limiting your income to those sources that prove how special you are.

In order to get over this self-limiting belief that your worth depends on your job, your brain needs new information. And the best, most direct way to experience this information is by receiving money even though you don't do anything to "deserve" it.

I recommend, therefore, that during the 30 days you make a very specific kind of investment. The point of this investment is not to make a lot of money over a long period of time. The point is not to dream that you could be rich "one day." Neither should you begin thinking of yourself as a "day trader" who works hard all day on making the right investments. Rather, the point is to let your money work *for you and then take the proceeds and immediately buy yourself a reward.* The amount you gain through this investment or the quality of the reward is completely irrelevant. You can earn $.79 and buy yourself a pack of gum. It does not matter. The point is to consciously give your mind new information. And the essence of this new information is this: You do not necessarily have to prove your worth by working for money. Money can work for you.

Of course, 30 days may not be enough time to earn any kind of return on an investment. You can at least start the process now, though. Perhaps the reward will come after the 30 days are over. Then again, you may surprise yourself. The Internet is full of investment opportunities. For modest fees you can open an account with an online trading company or you can do the same thing at your local bank. When you invest purely for fun, with the idea of receiving a little bit of extra money in the very near future, it will feel like a real possibility rather than an unreachable goal. You'll be more comfortable letting your money work to make you richer.

Step Fifteen: Hire Someone

I suggested in the last chapter that it's OK to be the boss. Now, you have an opportunity to do exactly that. You can create this experience for yourself through the simple act of hiring someone. Hiring another individual is a visceral way to experience your own fears around the issue of control: fear of being controlled; fear of controlling others; fear of losing control of the details of your life.

I'm not suggesting you hire a full-time employee necessarily. You may be struggling financially at this point and cannot afford it. Perhaps you do not need a full-time employee. Perhaps you do not need an employee at all. That is not the point. The point is to have the experience of being the boss, of taking responsibility for somebody else's actions.

If you consider yourself a member of the helping or creative professions, you are probably willing to let other people hire you. It's easy to think of yourself as an employee, independent contractor, or self-employed individual. It is much more of a stretch to think of yourself as an employer. Performing this exercise will help push you in that direction.

You can hire someone on a temporary basis. Even if it's only for a day or a few hours, the experience will serve to knock your mind out of its habitual patterns.

I'm not talking about contracting out a professional to perform a job. I'm talking about hiring someone who will follow you physically around and do what you tell him to do. Temporary agencies are a good place to look for day laborers. Or perhaps you know a student or unemployed person. As always, heed the rules or regulations that apply in your city or state.

Negotiate a pay scale with this individual. Give a detailed description of the job you need done. Perhaps you need a room painted or your garage cleaned out. After you've given directions, supervise the work. Make sure it is being done to your specifications. Take responsibility for the outcome of another human being's endeavors.

While you're in the midst of this exercise, feel what it's like to have somebody else dependent on you for direction. What kind of resistance does this arouse in your mind? Does it reveal parts of you that you do not like? What parts? Do you like being a boss? Are you afraid you like it too much? Are you afraid of becoming a tyrant? Just notice everything. Write it down in your journal.

Step Sixteen: Break with the Past

You're halfway through the program. Your mind may be rebelling a bit, just like my mind did in the Denver basement. You may have thrown your own symbolic peanut butter jar against the wall already. You may have yelled and screamed, "This is useless! I'm never going to change!"

But the truth is, and I think you'll agree by now, that you can change. You can Switch in an instant. The problem, unfortunately, is that if you have not yet Made the Switch, you feel exactly the same as you did at the beginning. I felt that I was 100 percent a Moonie right up until the second before I snapped. This is the way it will be for you, too. You will continue to feel 100 percent trapped inside the money-less bubble right up until the moment that you are no longer trapped. It is not a gradual escape.

Keep going.

In order to keep moving toward your own Switch, it is crucial that you break away from the patterns that have held you back for a long time. Unfortunately, many of these patterns were handed down to you by the people you are closest to, such as parents, spouses, and friends, which makes it especially difficult to break away. In order to start sending your brain a stream of new information regarding these patterns, reflect on the questions below. Then spend some time filling out your answers in your journal.

1. What did your mother teach you about money?

_____

_____

_____

_____

2. What did your father teach you about money?

_____

_____

_____

_____

3. How does your spouse, partner, or significant other feel about money? What are your main differences of opinion on the subject?

_____

_____

_____

_____

4. What influence have friends, relatives, and others had on your financial life? What advice have they given? What expectations do they have of you?

_____

_____

_____

_____

5. What do you imagine people say about your relationship with money when you are not around?

_____

_____

_____

_____

All of these influences have contributed to your present state of mind. They are part of your financial reality. Most likely, you are abiding by other people's values. You are listening to what has been told to you, agreeing with the common point of view. Over time, these influences have molded your reality. What you need to do is discard that reality and construct a new one. You need to build a new hologram inside your mind, but to do that you need to dismantle the old one. It's time to rebel.

As a symbol of your inner rebellion, write down the four most important items from the lists above. Which ones kept coming up again and again? What messages were repeatedly forced into your mind? Summarize each in a catchphrase of just a few words. For example, if you were taught to always have money on hand for an emergency, you might say, "Save for a rainy day." Write those phrases in the column on the left. Then, in the column on the right, craft your response. For example, if you discovered that both your father and your two closest friends continually advised you to "Get a good, safe job," you can rebel by saying, "Take an entrepreneurial risk."

Conventional Wisdom	Your Response
1. _____	_____
2. _____	_____
3. _____	_____
4. _____	_____
5. _____	_____

Step Seventeen: Lift Someone Up

Once you've Made the Switch, you'll feel an urge to help other people do the same. This is universally true. In fact, the one sure way to recognize somebody with a poverty mentality is by that person's desire to begrudge other people's success. If you try, as part of the

30-day program, to help other people reach their monetary goals, you will essentially "trick" your mind by giving it the message that you have already Made the Switch.

Lift someone up. Identify a specific individual, perhaps within your own circle of friends and colleagues, or somebody else you believe would benefit from your help, and then concentrate your energies on supporting that person's potential in life. This does not necessarily mean giving monetary support. In fact, giving money is probably counterproductive. There are, however, several actions that will have a powerful positive impact:

- Make a specific offer to help. Be straightforward, explain that you see the potential in this person, and then offer plenty of moral support and encouragement. Sit down and ask a lot of questions. Find out what needs to be done and make a plan to help.
- Spend time. Time is the most valuable offering you can give to another human being. Take all the time you need to get the full picture and decide what you can do that will be most helpful.
- Intervene on this person's behalf. Talk to somebody. Write a letter of recommendation. Call the right friends who can intercede. Help with a résumé, job application, or bank loan. Become this person's advocate. The more insight and information you can offer, the better.
- Follow up. Be there for your protégé as time goes on, well past the 30 days, and you'll continue to discover new ways to help, which will in turn give your mind more messages about how rich you already are.

If you do feel compelled to offer money, even a small amount, it is better to create a mini-charity in your name than to give funds directly to one person. Start a new account at your bank that will specifically support an individual or individuals who demonstrate their need and a sincere desire to improve their lives.

Step Eighteen: Give Back

Another trait common to those folks who Make the Switch is a sincere desire to give back to those who have helped them along the way. Now, it's your turn to give back.

Some person, institution, or profession helped you get where you are today. Even if you are unemployed and looking for a job, you can still identify something you are grateful for, and someone you are grateful to. Pick one source of your good fortune and show your appreciation by giving something back. This does not have to be a monetary gift, though that is common. If you don't have the money to give, simply send a letter of appreciation. Let people know that you care.

Rich people who have "arrived" are the ones who give back to those who have helped them. You can start to think of yourself as someone who has arrived, too. Give your mind that message by giving back.

Step Nineteen: Tithe

Tithing is an excellent way to give your mind the message that you have enough money to share with others. Traditionally, tithing meant giving 10 percent of your income, usually to the church. The root of the word tithe means "one-tenth," and this has been the standard for many years. I think this narrow definition keeps many people from benefiting others and themselves through tithing. You can donate less than 10 percent and still do a world of good.

If you do not already donate a certain amount of your income to a charity or religious organization, then start. The amount does not have to be large. It is not necessary to give a lot. It is only necessary to give. In fact, you may be tempted to give too much. Wealthy people in general donate a reasonable percentage of their income that doesn't affect their lifestyle. You can do the same thing. Give a reasonable amount to an organization with a mission that you believe in. Make sure the amount you give makes sense for your income (or your lack of income), and watch your money work. Gauge how it can most effectively help others. This is what the rich do. Make a Switch to acting that way, too.

Step Twenty: Befriend a Rich Person

You can read all the get-rich books in the world, listen to all the motivational tapes, and watch all the videos featuring wise and wealthy teachers, but until you meet a real-life wealthy teacher yourself, everything will remain theoretical. You've got to make it real. You've got to befriend a rich person.

Most parables like *The Instant Millionaire, The Alchemist,* and *The Greatest Salesman in the World* are really about getting to know a rich person and learning his or her secrets. The *Millionaire Next Door,* the *Millionaire Mind, Cracking the Millionaire Code, The One Minute Millionaire,* and countless others all attempt to familiarize readers with what it feels like to befriend a rich mentor. That's their essence. These books give you the experience second-hand, but why not experience the reality?

I suggest you identify a person whose lifestyle you admire, someone who has the time and ambition to pursue her passion and make an impact in the world, then get to know her. This person does not need to be a multimillionaire, but she should be living a rich lifestyle free of nagging money concerns. The type of car she drives doesn't matter. The neighborhood she lives in is irrelevant. What matters is that she is financially free.

Of course, it is difficult to build a true friendship in 30 days, but you can at least make a start. How? In my case, I had a client who was willing. She and her husband are worth hundreds of millions of dollars and lead busy lives, yet she took the time to befriend me. I've gone to workshops at Omega Institute with her, cruised on her yacht, stayed in her homes, traveled on her jets. And we've spent many hours talking about my plans and goals. This mentoring is still going on today, and it continues to help me learn. In my case, this rich friend has turned out to be my mentor, too. See step number 6 in this program.

You may find that the most likely place to seek a wealthy friend is among your clients. Or, you may think about volunteering for a charity where many rich individuals spend time. The most important thing is to dismantle the reverse-prejudice you have in your mind against the rich. The moment you drop your judgments, someone will be there available to teach you. When the student is ready, the rich friend will appear.

Truly rich people who have Made the Switch are willing to teach other people and share their knowledge. They are generous. Their minds operate in a field of unlimited possibilities. They know that by teaching and uplifting you, they are uplifting themselves. When you're inside the moneyless bubble, you subconsciously separate yourself from rich people. When you befriend someone you perceive as rich, you begin to break down this barrier and destroy the bubble. You get closer to making the Switch.

Step Twenty-One: Give to the Rich

With all due respect to Robin Hood, I'd like to suggest that, at least during this 30-day program, you give to the rich as well as the poor. Giving something to a rich person, in fact, is one of the best ways to befriend her.

It may be a little awkward to simply fork over some cash, so instead you may want to give a thoughtful gift. Another technique I've used is to invite a rich person to lunch or dinner. Pick up the tab. This takes you out of the subconsciously subservient role you may be playing. When people, including you, expect you will *not* pick up the tab, paying for lunch can be a real eye opener. This act itself—the lifting of the check and the extracting of the money from your wallet or pocketbook—can really push you toward making the Switch. Observe your reactions carefully when you're doing it. Pay attention to your raised heart rate, your nervousness. How do you feel? Keep asking yourself why you are feeling this way. These are the kinds of questions a deprogrammer asks.

This simple exercise will help you break down the authoritarian structures in your brain that habitually place somebody else above you. Don't let others always take the advantage by paying your way. Give to the rich. It will lift you up.

Step Twenty-Two: Take an Acting Class

Taking an improv acting class during your 30-day program is a great idea for two reasons. First of all, it will improve your ability to get others to respond to you. For better or for worse, when you're interacting with other people, your body is your instrument. If you learn how to use it well, you will be more effective in all areas of your life. Chances are you are quite unaware of how your body and voice are perceived by others. This makes it difficult to create your desired effect, whether it is to show strength, competency, authority, or any other positive attribute. Actors are experts at projecting certain states of being.

You may have noticed that leaders are usually people willing to stand in front of others. To be seen, you must be visible. And to be effective, your presence must have a purpose. Acting teaches you how to project your purpose.

Second, and more importantly, an acting class will teach you how you can act like a "bad" person. This was the biggest benefit in my own case. When my acting teacher saw me try to portray an evil villain in the act of robbing a bank in front of the class, he stopped everything and said, "You're a really nice person, aren't you?"

"Yes," I replied, unsure what he was getting at.

"Well," he said, "It's time to get over yourself. Go ahead, man, get mean. Let it out."

What happened next was a revelation. Right there in front of the whole class I became a slimy, evil person. It was like Jekyll and Hyde. How was this possible? I had always been taught to be a good, nice, kind, and compassionate person. My teacher showed me how to let go of that self-definition and feel what it was like to be "bad." It was pretty profound. I understood, in that moment of acting, that I did have the potential for self-centered evil actions. I had a bad side! It might sound silly, but this was a profoundly freeing realization.

After taking that class, I no longer felt the need to prove to anyone, or myself, how good I was. I viscerally felt how I was indeed a good person. And I also felt how I was bad. I no longer had the need to push one reality away in order to prove the other.

By always acting good and dedicating your whole career to being a caring, compassionate, artistic, creative individual, you are also pushing a little of your innate bad, selfish, destructive side into the background. You're covering up your shadow. This takes energy. Free that energy up by releasing your inner bad person.

Of course, it's not a good idea to actually go out and rob a bank, just to prove that you have an evil side. Taking an acting class, on the other hand, is a safe way to give yourself a truly mind-opening experience. Improv acting, in particular, will give you the opportunity to explore and expand your own range of emotions and self-concepts "in the moment."

And don't worry. Playing the part of a murderer on stage will not inspire you to go out and kill someone. You've already proven to yourself and the world that you are, at heart, one of the "good guys." This little exercise will help you stretch the limitations of that good person. It may help you nurture your lean and mean side, in order to help your good side survive and thrive.

The less inclined you are to take an acting workshop, the more effective it will be for you to do so, and the bigger Switch it can potentially make in your life. You do not have to enroll at Julliard and pursue a career on stage or screen. Find a one- or two-day workshop, or longer if you're so inclined. Check the Yellow Pages or the Internet for classes in your area.

Step Twenty-Three: Become a Speaker

Did you know that the biggest fear among most people is public speaking? This fear is stronger than the fear of death itself. So, as comedian Jerry Seinfeld said, if you have to go to a funeral, you'd be better off in the casket than giving the eulogy.

Why is public speaking such a huge universal fear? There are many explanations, but I believe the root cause is biological. This primordial fear has been a part of the human race for eons. Think about it: When you give a speech, you're standing in front of many people, all of whom are staring at you expectantly. Those eyeballs are tracking your every move, stalking you. Throughout history, what was the only reason a human being would be stalked like this? That's right— if he were being hunted!

The reason you're so terrified of public speaking is that you're afraid the audience is going to tear you limb from limb and eat you alive. I know, it sounds like a ridiculous exaggeration. But think about it. Why else would you feel such utter dread at the thought of simply talking to other human beings?

Public speaking is one of the most direct routes to increasing your prosperity. If you can overcome this basic fear, you will be able to more effectively communicate your message to others, explain your vision, ask for support, teach what you've learned, and lead others in pursuit of their dreams. No better way exists to upgrade your chances at success.

The tremendous fear you may feel at the thought of public speaking can be a great tool to help you move toward making the Switch. If you put yourself in that intense situation in front of other people, your heart rate will go up and your adrenal glands will release a flood of energy into your system. Your senses will be heightened and your mind will be placed on high alert. In this state, the new stream of information coming into your brain will be greatly magnified. Use this to your advantage.

Make the decision to move consciously through your fear. What you will find, if you allow the energy to stream through your body, is that your personal power will increase. Those people who face their fears are the ones who get recognized. Believe it or not, other people will be desperate to recognize you and raise you onto a pedestal. They will be rooting for you while you're standing in front of them on the stage because they're relieved it's you up there instead of them.

Even though this experience feels extremely intense, it is basically quite safe. After all, you're not really going to be eaten alive. The worst that could happen is that you do not do as well as you'd hoped. In which case you can try again. The energy will always be there to help you. Most people never get over their nervousness, and that's a good thing. It's what propels you to do your best each time.

As part of my own program, I joined the National Speakers Association (NSA), attended their conferences, learned from their teachers, and advanced my career by becoming a professional speaker at seminars and workshops. I continue to expand this aspect of my career and am now moving into expert witness work in courtroom trials.

You don't need to take professional speaking to this extreme, but during the 30 days, I suggest that you investigate the NSA (www.nsaspeaker.org) and Toastmasters International (www.toastmasters.org). Toastmasters has local groups around the world where you can go and develop your speaking abilities either inexpensively or free of charge in a supportive environment. If this is not possible, I suggest setting up your own speaking engagement. The topic can be anything you believe in and know something about. If you've gained just a slight mastery of any topic or technique, you know more about it than 99 percent of the general public. Invite people you know or put up fliers at local stores. I once spoke at a Barnes & Noble bookstore when there were just two people in the audience—my mother and father. It was embarrassing and difficult, and I felt horrible at the time, but I did it. Now I speak to thousands of people all across North America. You can, too. For inspiration, check out Dottie Walters' book, *Speak and Grow Rich*.

Do it. Speak. Grow.

Step Twenty-Four: Pay Attention to the Money

Face it. You think numbers are about the most boring thing on the planet. Sure, you'd like to think of yourself as numerically competent, but it's hard to engage with something as cold, logical, and inhuman as a calculation. If you are reading this book, you are, by definition, a people person. And people people care more about passion, interaction, and emotion. They are not, usually, stimulated by a balance sheet.

You need to remedy this situation. The best way to do this is to get involved in a numbers-oriented project that has a direct impact on your own fiscal well-being. I suggest you create a special 30-day budget during this program. A simple table like the one on page 127 will suffice to keep track of this. Write down every dollar that comes in and every dollar that goes out. If you have not done this before, it may amaze you to see the numbers add up. You may not be aware of where your money is going.

If you have difficulty focusing your mind on this exercise, ask yourself why. Why is it difficult to focus on your money? Why do you react against keeping track of the details? Focusing your mind on money in this manner is a way to deprogram your mind from its habitual pattern of not focusing on money. If you want to take this process a step further, invest in a computerized budget software program such as Quicken™. Filling out the information in this pro-

DATE	INCOME	SOURCE	EXPENSE	PURCHASE	TYPE
	$		$		CASH/CHECK/CC
	$		$		CASH/CHECK/CC
	$		$		CASH/CHECK/CC
	$		$		CASH/CHECK/CC
	$		$		CASH/CHECK/CC
	$		$		CASH/CHECK/CC
	$		$		CASH/CHECK/CC
	$		$		CASH/CHECK/CC
	$		$		CASH/CHECK/CC
	$		$		CASH/CHECK/CC
	$		$		CASH/CHECK/CC
	$		$		CASH/CHECK/CC
	$		$		CASH/CHECK/CC
TOTALS	$		$		

gram and keeping track of it will force your mind into new patterns that will help you Make the Switch.

Step Twenty-Five: Dream

Some of the most successful people in the world set time aside every day specifically to nurture their creativity. They reserve a certain period to do nothing but brainstorm on the bigger issues because they know that simply reacting to the same old problems and concerns on a daily basis will keep them stuck in their present reality. In order for your mind to Switch to a new reality, you have to consistently feed it new possibilities.

During these 30 days, find time to dream. Some people prefer to take a long solo walk on the beach or in the mountains. Some prefer a quiet room without distractions. Others find time in their cars during a long drive. Turn the radio off. Strip away outside distractions. Separate yourself from your routine. Dream.

You should focus your dreaming on those problems or situations that seem to be keeping you stuck. Then, vividly imagine yourself as having overcome those obstacles and getting unstuck. Go back and forth repeatedly between the reality and the vision, until you create tension between the two. Let the tension simmer. Think of nothing else.

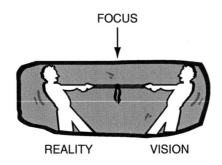

Where to focus your dreaming

In your journal, keep track of the thoughts that come to you through dreaming and brainstorming. Doing so will help you access the field of infinite possibilities in your mind. Remember, the rich you is already there, waiting to be recognized. All you have to do is tune in to the new frequency. Dreaming will help you get there.

Step Twenty-Six: Be Totally Selfish

Choose one full day of the 30 and practice the art of being selfish. You may think this suggestion is ridiculous, or you may throw your arms up in celebration at the idea. Believe me, it is much harder than it sounds. Since you are one of the "good" people and you've dedicated your livelihood to helping others and expressing your spirit, you will quite likely find it difficult to focus exclusively on yourself and your own egotistical needs for a day.

If necessary, let other people know what you're doing so you won't offend them, and then, for just this day, do nothing for anybody else. Treat yourself to a spa visit. Lie in bed and read. Don't answer the phone. Cook no meals. Meet no deadlines. Engage in your favorite creative pursuit. Paint. Draw. Write in your journal. Watch your favorite movies on DVD. Don't do a single thing you *need* to do.

You may find it impossible to go through the entire day without feeling guilty about your self-indulgence. That's OK. Guilt is precisely the state you want to cultivate in this exercise. As soon as you feel guilt start to creep in, stop and pay attention to your thoughts and the feelings in your body. Just sit or lie down, take some deep breaths, and observe the sensations. What is it about focusing on yourself that makes you cringe with guilt? Why does your sense of self-worth, even for just a few hours, depend so utterly on being other-oriented?

Circle of Guilt

Do you see how you've created a vicious circle in your life? If you believe your choice of livelihood somehow proves your worth, you have to keep working at it all the time. If you stop, for even one day, the self-feedback loop sputters. Your mind stops receiving the constant stream of information it needs to hold its reality together. You start to get the feeling that you are "falling short" of your vision for yourself. Guilt kicks in as a self-regulating mechanism.

Take a look at Money Myth number 4 in Chapter Two again. It concerns the need to confess your sins of self-indulgence. During this one day, try to break the circuit of guilt and confession. Go beyond striving. Embrace the selfish part of your nature, with no need to make excuses for it. This is difficult, but it will push your mind forcefully toward making the Switch.

Step Twenty-Seven: Read, Watch & Listen

During the 30 days, read this book over again. In addition, read other books and magazines that support your intentions and focus your mind on making the Switch. Bombard yourself with new streams of information. You might take a look at the books I've been referring to, which are listed in the back, under Resources.

Also, listen to tapes, CDs, or MP3s that help you stay on track. Watch DVDs and seminar recordings about finances, abundance, setting goals, and defining your life's purpose. You might even consider attending a live seminar event.

When I was deprogrammed from the Moonies, I had to be force-fed a lot of new information in order to get my mind out of its rut. This is what you must do, too. If you read, watch, and listen to the right things, this process will be accelerated.

Step Twenty-Eight: Join a Community

If you go around telling people that you are trying to Make the Switch to Being Rich, they might look at you like you're crazy. After reading this book, the concept makes a certain amount of sense to you, but many people will have no idea what you're talking about. What's worse, certain people, especially friends and family, may have a vested interest in keeping you from improving your economic situation. It may be a subconscious desire on their part, hidden beneath layers of encouragement and support, but when it comes right down to it, they're happy with you the way you are. In fact, they're happier with you than you are with yourself. Your ongoing position inside the moneyless bubble provides them companionship and predictability.

During these 30 days, you can accelerate your move toward a Switch by choosing to spend time with like-minded individuals. Hang out with other people who are also stretching their boundaries and trying to break through to another level. It will inspire you.

If you don't know anybody who shares your desire to break through limiting beliefs and expand prosperity, you can purposefully try to find someone. Good places to search are at prosperity workshops and seminars. If you have the funds, think about hiring a personal coach. You might also consider asking your mentor to join your group of "prosperity partners." Share meals with this dream team. Talk about your plans, goals, and challenges. When it comes to making the Switch, you'll find that the power of like-minded company will greatly magnify your own individual willpower.

Step Twenty-Nine: Take a Retreat

Set aside one of your 30 days and turn it into a retreat. Go someplace. Get away from your usual surroundings. Then concentrate for the entire day on nothing else. Put all of the components of this program together. Dream. Write in your journal. Read, watch, and listen to inspiring materials. Join with your "prosperity partners" and focus on nothing else. In my own case, I locked myself in a room with two like-minded friends at the local Embassy Suites for an entire weekend. We listened over and over again to prosperity tapes. We focused all of our energy on our goal. We didn't sleep much. We ordered room service.

This kind of intense immersion simulates the deprogramming experience I had in that Denver basement. It is a good idea to schedule it near the end of your 30 days so you are already familiar with all of the steps and can review the progress you've made.

Step Thirty: Go For It!

The last step in this program is actually the first. I am asking you, right here and right now, to step up and actually begin.

Faced with all the challenges presented in this chapter, you may be thinking to yourself, "Well, I'm not really doing that bad, am I? At least I'm not living on the street. I have an interesting, comfortable life. Maybe all this trouble just isn't worth it."

This is a trap. It is your mind's habitual patterns surfacing again. Believe me, your mind is terrified of change. It will take a catastrophe to make it happen. And in the meantime you will cower in the basement, slinking around, trying to avoid the powerful deprogrammer who gets in your face and won't let you look away, forcing you to think.

"Think, robot! Think!" Ted Patrick shouted at me. And I'm yelling those words out to you now, too.

It is crucial that you perform the steps, not just read them. I could have read Ted Patrick's book, but if I had not spent time with him in that basement, I probably never would have left the Moonies. I'd still be a mindless robot today, selling flowers on the streets.

You owe it to yourself to take a risk. It's time to make a change. It is the nature of humans to change and expand, just like the universe changes and expands, or businesses change and expand. This is the secret that many rich people already know. Being rich is not a static state. It is not the end condition of a finite process. Making the Switch doesn't mean you reach a new level and then stop. It doesn't mean you've reached your goal. It means you are operating from a different perspective that offers new opportunities. It means you've moved from a contracting state to an expansive state. This, in turn, makes reaching your goals possible.

If you don't go for it now, then when? The timing is never perfect. You never know how things are going to turn out if you jump in right this minute. But there is one thing you can know for sure: The opportunity presented in this particular moment will never be here again.

Go ahead. Don't lose this chance. What have you got to lose by engaging yourself fully in this program? Look at the 30 steps again. Choose the one thing that feels most difficult, challenging, or scary. Take a deep breath. Then . . . Go for it!

Let me know how you do. Visit www.makingtheswitchtobeingrich.com and tell me your story. I'd love to hear it.

Here is a list of the 30 items in your self-deprogramming program. You can use it for easy reference, checking each item off as it's completed.

#	STEP	✓	NOTES
1	KIDNAP YOUR BRAIN		
2	LOCK YOUR BRAIN IN THE BASEMENT		
3	WATCH YOUR LANGUAGE		
4	DISCIPLINE YOURSELF		
5	STOP COMPLAINING		
6	CHOOSE A NEW LEADER		
7	MAKE A CHOICE		
8	MAKE A COMMITMENT		
9	INCORPORATE YOURSELF		

10	MAKE ONE THING		
11	SELL ONE THING		
12	DISTRIBUTE ONE THING		
13	THANK PEOPLE FOR THE MONEY		
14	INVEST IN SOMETHING		
15	HIRE SOMEONE		
16	BREAK WITH THE PAST		
17	LIFT SOMEONE UP		
18	GIVE BACK		
19	TITHE		
20	BEFRIEND A RICH PERSON		
21	GIVE TO THE RICH		
22	TAKE AN ACTING CLASS		
23	BECOME A SPEAKER		
24	PAY ATTENTION TO THE MONEY		
25	DREAM		
26	BE TOTALLY SELFISH		
27	READ, WATCH & LISTEN		
28	JOIN A COMMUNITY		
29	TAKE A RETREAT		
30	GO FOR IT!		

Of course, not all of these steps are appropriate for everybody. What if you're already comfortable with selling? Or you've already mastered public speaking? You can mix and match the 30 suggestions to suit your own situation, customizing a program that makes sense for you. Ted Patrick did the same thing for each one of his clients. The underlying principle was the same. He kept feeding new information into the system and kept asking challenging questions to open people's minds. Then he presented another plausible reality, until the person started to listen and eventually snapped out of his robot-like trance.

When I snapped in front of that class in Dallas, I finally "tuned into" abundance. It happened in an instant, like tuning into a new station on the radio. All it took was the turn of a dial, the push of a button, the flick of a Switch. When you tune into a new station, it's instantaneous because the radio waves are already there in the air. All a radio does is access different frequencies. Your brain, through the reality-structuring mechanisms you learned about in Chapter Six, is capable of tuning into different frequencies also. Abundance is already streaming all around you, like 103.5 FM. You're just not tuned into it yet.

You never know when it's going to happen to you. Perhaps it will be during the course of these 30 days. I hope so, but if it does not happen now, I urge you to keep going forward with your own plans, following your own visions. Eventually, it will happen for you, too. You might not even recognize the precise moment as it occurs. I didn't know, during my impassioned speech in Dallas, that I had Made the Switch. That came later in the weekend, when I tallied up the total sales and realized they were $9,000.

It doesn't matter how "smart" you are or what other people say you can or cannot achieve. It doesn't matter what grades the schools gave you. Most successful people have been told at one time or another that they didn't have what it takes to succeed, but they took that information as a challenge. They defied conventional wisdom and overcame any shortcomings they might have had. This is the process that you too can begin by facing the challenges in the 30-day program.

On the deepest level, Making the Switch is about reuniting with yourself. About trusting yourself. About letting go of the need for somebody else to be the authority in your life. You are the ultimate authority on you. You are the expert. You can make your own choices, take responsibility for your own feelings, and decide what's best. When you Make the Switch, you maximize the number of people you can help by using your natural talents and skills, while at the same time living a full, exciting, rich life.

Is there any more important pursuit?

> *"We make a living by what we get, but we make a life by what we give."*
> Winston Churchill

Doing Well While Doing Good

How will you know when you've actually Made the Switch? It's not a matter of knowing, really, but of doing. You already know what you need to do in order to be rich. You've known for a long time. When you Make the Switch, you go beyond just knowing and start to take action. You destroy the blocks in your mind that have held you back from doing what you know you need to do.

- You KNOW you need to pay yourself first.
- You KNOW you need to stop overspending on credit.
- You KNOW you need to increase your self-confidence and become more of a leader.
- You KNOW you need to become more entrepreneurial.
- You KNOW you could become better at uplifting and inspiring others.
- You KNOW you need to give to those less fortunate than you.

- You KNOW you need to create something of value and sell it to people who will benefit by it.
- You KNOW you've got to make a firm choice, follow your vision, and make a commitment to stick to it for the long run.
- You KNOW you should discipline yourself and use your precious time and resources more wisely.
- You KNOW you should stop complaining and take responsibility for your own life.
- You already KNOW everything.

But life is more than merely knowing. You've got to believe. Until you Make the Switch, your current beliefs (the habitual patterns of your brain brought about by subconscious conditioning) will keep you from acting on what you already know. Between the knowledge and the action there exists an invisible barrier. This barrier is your programmed Robot self. Until you are deprogrammed, the barrier will always be there. My hope is that this book will help you remove the barrier.

You have noticed, no doubt, that this book does not give you a recipe for going out and making money. It is not a manual about investing in the stock market. It does not include any tips about buying and selling real estate. What it does do, I hope, is make it possible for other books and other techniques to work, should you try to use them. The reason you may not have found success with other programs in the past is that your mind was not prepared to accept the consequences of following the advice they offered. If you had followed their advice successfully, you would have been rich by now. But your mind was not prepared to be rich. You had not Made the Switch yet. And, when it comes right down to it, you didn't care enough about making money for its own sake. Sure, you want to be doing well, but you also want to be doing good. You want to make an excellent living and maybe even get rich, but only if you can also follow a path that has heart and meaning. That's what this final chapter is about.

After my deprogramming, I stayed with my parents for a few months before moving out on my own again. It felt good to be leading a normal life and I enjoyed my freedom, but still I felt somehow empty. Even though the Moonies used brainwashing techniques to trick me into working for them, at least they had given me a compelling reason to get up every morning. Being part of a team that thinks it is saving the world is highly motivating! Now, what was I supposed to do?

After the initial excitement of homecoming had worn off, I tried several alternatives to fill the void. First, I accompanied a friend to a fundamentalist Christian retreat in the woods of central Florida. Then I visited a yoga center in rural Pennsylvania. These pursuits, I eventually realized, were leading me away from taking ultimate responsibility for my own life. I was still seeking spiritual permission from an outside authority. While I don't deny that these paths are perfect avenues of self-expression for many people, I was seeking something else. What I wanted, even though I was only dimly aware of it at first, was a way to express my spirit and creativity through my life's work.

Like many people seeking to prepare themselves for a career, I went back to school. I scrambled to get good grades so that I would be hired by a good company and find my own niche in the "real" world. I graduated with honors. I worked for some good companies. But this, too, was ultimately unfulfilling.

Finally, I sat down for a talk with the one person who had been there for me all along. He was quiet most of the time, only offering support when I asked for it, but at that crucial moment in Denver he had taken decisive action and had saved me from a life of mental captivity and exploitation.

"Dad, I'm not sure if you can help me now," I stammered one night in his living room. He shut the TV off and gave me his full attention.

"What is it, son?"

"I guess I'm trying to figure out what I'm supposed to do with the rest of my life. I can't just work at some pointless job. I've got to believe in what I'm doing. At least when I lived with the Moonies, I had something to believe in. Now . . ."

He looked at me with fondness, as he always did, but this time there was a little sadness in his eyes, too.

"It was a hard decision for your mother and me to hire Ted Patrick," he said. "We weren't completely sure it was the right thing. You definitely believed strongly in what you were doing, and we didn't want to interfere with the choices you were making. But one thing convinced us to call Patrick."

"What was it?"

"We know you pretty well, son, and we could see that you weren't yourself. You didn't seem free, and that's the one thing we've always wanted for you. Freedom doesn't guarantee you easy answers. In fact, it pretty much assures there won't be easy answers. You've got to find your own answers and figure out what to believe in as you go along."

"What do you believe in, Dad?" I'd wanted to ask him that question for a long time, but I was afraid of what he might say. I was afraid that he actually believed in nothing, that he felt as unfulfilled as I did, and that he had no real answers for me.

"I believe in you, Steve," he said without hesitation.

At that moment, I realized what he must have gone through, how traumatic it must have been to kidnap his own son, to take the risk of losing me forever. He wasn't just mouthing empty words. He took action. He meant it. He believed in me.

Lessons From the Land of Floating

My father's words gave me the strength to believe in myself and follow my own dreams. Still, it didn't happen overnight. I continued to experience more of what Ted Patrick called "floating." You, too, may find yourself floating for a while, even after you've Made the Switch. This is not necessarily a bad thing. It takes time to assemble all the parts of a unique, independent life. You have to cultivate your new freedom carefully. As you forge your own authentic existence through this floating period, it will help if you keep the following ten points in mind.

1. Continue to Stay in Shape.

As I mentioned before, Moonies' eyes, voices, and bodies change when they are under the control of the group. Men get flabby and glassy-eyed. Women even lose their periods. When I snapped out of the group, my body started to change back to that of a normal, healthy person, but it took time. When you Make the Switch out of your own poverty consciousness, you will experience a physical change too, though it will probably be more subtle than mine was. You will walk and talk with more confidence. The way you stand will change, especially when you are in public. Your posture will improve a little. Your thought processes will be different, and this will influence the way you look. You'll be a changed person.

When I returned home after my deprogramming, I couldn't do a single pull-up. I remembered Ted Patrick's good example with his pushups and his vigorous presence, and I decided to go on a serious exercise program. Gradually, I made my flabby Moonie body strong and healthy once more. I decided to make this a lifelong commitment. You'll find the same commitment has been made by CEOs, entrepreneurs, entertainers, and other people with a mission to fulfill. Your body is your instrument. Your health is irreplaceable. What good will riches do if you're not strong and healthy to enjoy them?

2. Continue to Develop Long-range Projects.

Just because you Make the Switch doesn't mean people are going to start walking up and handing you buckets full of cash. Doors will open, but you still have to walk through them. It's important that you continue to develop long-range projects, things that you believe in that will eventually create revenue streams for you, even if there is more work (and less reward) at the beginning. In my case, I developed book ideas and eventually published them. Making the Switch did not mean that publishers suddenly showered me with money. It meant that I had the confidence to create something that publishers would take seriously and invest their precious dollars in. You too have some long-range plans you can continue to work on over time. With the confidence that comes with your new state of mind, you will be more likely to succeed now, even if you've tried a similar project in the past and it didn't work out.

3. Continue to Look for Financing Opportunities for your Long-term Goals.

Another thing that will happen when you Make the Switch is that you'll feel more confident about asking other people to invest in your ideas. Cultivate several resources that you'll be able to turn to when the time is right to move forward with a plan. Whether these resources are friends, families, institutions or strangers, you've got to create a proven track record so people will trust you. Take out small loans at first, and pay them back in a timely manner. Make it your business to build your credibility. It will come in handy one day.

4. Continue to Grow your Circle of Friends.

Expand your network of creative, inspired, and active friends from many walks of life. Your new rich friend/mentor may introduce you to other new associates. The more people you know, especially within your chosen field, the better. The adage "It's who you know" is absolutely true. You should spend at least 20 percent of your available time cultivating your networking base by attending functions, taking the time to get to know people and their families, and schmoozing in general. "Connectors" are people who put other people together, and they are the most valuable links in any chain. Continue to develop your own ability to connect.

5. Continue to Work with your Mentor.

No matter how successful you become, it's important to keep yourself humble by constantly seeking out the advice and inspiration of people more accomplished or experienced than you are. Keep in touch with your mentor or find new mentors as often as necessary. Sometimes a mentorship will last just one day or an hour. You could benefit by the counsel of a series of mentors over time. You'll always find something to learn from the people who show up at different stages of your life.

6. Continue to do the Scariest Thing First.

At each point along your path, even after you've Made the Switch, you will continue to encounter roadblocks. The most effective way to handle them is head-on. Choose the one thing that seems most difficult or intimidating, then plunge forward into it. If you don't, you'll be spending mental energy trying to avoid it.

It's a mistake to think things will be easy if you are rich. Just ask any rich person. The types of problems and challenges you face change, but they will still be there. Make a habit of dealing with these challenges. No matter where you are on your economic journey, this habit will benefit you greatly.

7. Continue to Look for Opportunities to Speak.

Get out there and make yourself visible. Continue to overcome the natural fear of speaking in public. If you take this risk, you gain leverage over all those other people who continue to sit back and listen. You'll continue to find many new opportunities to speak, whether at community meetings, educational events, social gatherings, conferences, or on video or DVD. The more speaking you do, the easier it gets. And even if it doesn't get any less scary, at the very least, you get accustomed to the fear. Over the years, I've continued to cultivate the speaking aspect of my career, to the point where now that is mostly what I do. Speaking in front of people and offering them everything I know is a service. It is also a great way to make money. In fact, I've found public speaking to be so important, I flew to California and took a three-day class called "Building Your Speaking and Writing Empire," from the authors of the *Chicken Soup for the Soul* series.

8. Continue to ask for More.

Even if you remain at a position that is perhaps not your dream job, you still have opportunities for growth. You can ask for a raise, but the best way to expand your earning potential in your current job is to dedicate yourself 100 percent to making the company successful, even though it is not your company or your vision. This doesn't work all the time, and you're bound to get discouraged now and again. But if you can continue to act that way on a consistent basis, you will stand a better chance at receiving more recognition and more money. If your present employer doesn't reward your dedication, then someone else will. You will move up.

If you're an independent contractor, your customers are the ones who can give you a raise. But the only way they'll give you more money is if you ask for it. Practice asking for more periodically. I tell my massage therapy students to determine the fee they are most comfortable charging for their services, and then ask for $5 more. It's not a lot, but little increments like this make all the difference over time. You can try something similar in your own field. Determine what is comfortable and then expand it a little at a time.

9. Continue to be a Leader.

When you Make the Switch, you begin operating from a new frame of reference in which you no longer feel the need for an authority figure to tell you how things are. In fact, you realize that you could take on the role of authority figure if you wanted to. I think that's a good idea, as long as you continue to seek such authority for the right reasons. If you're reading this book, chances are that you've dedicated yourself to uplifting, inspiring, helping, and connecting with other people. Your prime motivation is not to achieve authority over them. This is precisely why you may be the best person to wield authority. Do not avoid this responsibility when it arises.

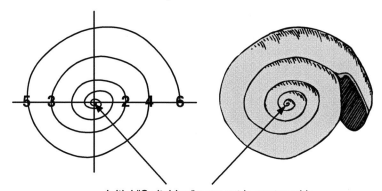

Initial "Switching" moment in center with
subsequent "mini switches" numbered on graph

10. Continue to Make More Switches.

Once you Make the Switch, you will not suddenly find yourself in a static, unchanging situation. Life will continue to be fluid and dynamic. You will have to keep changing, too. If you resist this, you are resisting the growth process that is a natural part of life. You can think of Switching in terms of a spiral. Once you make your initial Switch, you establish your mind in a new pattern and start to perceive things in a new way. This is the center of the spiral shown in the drawing. But then you continue to grow within that new pattern and continue to have realizations, or "mini-switches," along the way, numbered 2–6 on the spiral.

You stay centered within the same new perceptive framework, but you grow organically, like a nautilus (shown on the right side of the drawing). Your new understanding spirals outward, like seashells, flowers, or galaxies, which also expand in a perfectly proportioned spiral form. Over time, you add incrementally to the initial realization you had when you first Made the Switch. You understand more as you grow. Don't resist this. In spite of the challenges, difficulties, and uncertainties ahead, keep growing. As my father said, your authentic path is not the one with easy answers, but it is the only one that will keep you in that ever-expansive state that your heart yearns to experience.

So, once you've deprogrammed yourself from your old patterns and made it successfully through your floating stage, what are the next steps? How, exactly, are you supposed to pursue your new rich life? My advice, at least at first, is to keep doing what you're already doing. In order to become successful with integrity, you must continue to pursue goals that are aligned with your dreams and deepest desires. I've written this book specifically for you because you're the type of person who needs to remain inspired by your life. What you do has to make a difference. Without that, what's the use of riches?

I'm here to inspire you to continue following your calling and to expand upon it, so that you can keep doing what you're good at and what gives you meaning, but in such a way that it also makes you *Rich*. Notice that the name of this book is not Making the Switch to Being a Millionaire. Being a millionaire does not make you Rich, at least not by my definition. I believe that being Rich means you're free to pursue the life you were meant to pursue. It means you are not trapped into doing somebody else's bidding simply because you haven't examined other possibilities within your own mind.

I have four basic suggestions for you to follow in the real world as you pursue your dreams:

1. Expand within your niche
2. Get rich to support your niche
3. Find an aligned niche
4. Discover new niches

Expand Within Your Niche

You already know what your heart is calling you to do. Perhaps you're already doing it. Or you're being drawn in that direction. Your instincts are tugging you toward a future you may not fully visualize yet, but you're a person with a "calling." Another word for this calling is "niche."

Whatever your niche is in this world, that is where you feel most compelled to be and are happiest. I suggest you stay somewhere within this niche, if it is possible to also find a way to make more money within it. This is what I have done.

I became a massage therapist a year after I left college. It didn't seem like a way to make a huge sum of money at the time, but it was what I felt called to do. I wanted to help, to literally touch people's lives, to uplift them, relax them, get them in touch with their own bodies—in short, to connect with them. Like many people in this profession, I eventually found myself struggling to make a good living. I needed to either find a new niche or expand my capacity to make money within the niche I loved.

I decided to expand. What I found was a vast support network already in place for people like me who wanted to grow and expand within their niches. These networks exist for people in many professions. Wherever you find yourself working, you can find a way to make much more money without forsaking your calling.

You have to be willing to grow, however. Often, this means letting go of the need to demonstrate your worth through the hands-on skills you learned to join your niche in the first place. You must be willing to develop new skills. You may have watched as other people in your niche have done exactly what you believe you are capable of doing. You see the leaders, the people whose names are known, the ones who have created something that your colleagues find useful. How have they done this?

Chances are, the people who move onto greater success within their niches have made a Switch of some kind. They can see things from a new perspective and therefore take advantage of the support network that already exists for their potential success. The following list covers some, but not all, of the paths that people pursue when they expand:

Consulting: As you gain knowledge and experience in your niche, you become a valuable resource for other people. Consultants charge others for the benefit of their knowledge and experience. Many good books offer details about setting up a consulting business within your niche.

Writing: Writing for trade magazines, journals, research texts, newsletters, e-books, and books is an excellent way to expand your potential within your niche. Although it is not as romantic as getting your best-selling novel made into a Hollywood movie, getting your information-filled book turned into a text used by others in your niche can indeed make you rich. I know many people in my own little massage niche who make a very good living from royalties alone.

Teaching/Training: Teaching is not usually regarded as a surefire path toward riches, but a certain kind of teaching can be extremely rewarding financially. I'm talking about workshops and seminars. If you can develop and package useful information in a short format (usually a weekend) that offers continuing-education credits in your field, people will pay good money for it.

Organizing: The other people in your niche need a way to organize themselves. This is usually accomplished through conventions, conferences, retreats, symposia, and similar group meetings, usually run through professional associations. What you may not realize is that the people who run the associations often make much more money than the members who join the associations. In the same way, people who raise the funds that help organize your profession may well be making more money than those who use the funds for research and other programs. If you learn how to help organize the people in your niche, you stand a good chance at becoming rich. At the same time, you'll be contributing to the field you love.

Speaking: Here it is again. You will have a much better chance at expanding within your niche if you develop the ability to speak in public. To organize others, teach seminars, or offer consultations, you need to hone your speaking skills. Keep at it.

Developing Products: Discover or invent a product that other professionals in your field will love to use, and then develop it. You know better than outsiders what your colleagues want and need. Start small, do not overextend your finances in pursuing this product, and stay focused within your niche. In my own massage niche, for example, the owner of the company that now makes the best-selling brand of oils and creams started out making products in the garage and delivering them by hand.

Developing Systems: You can create a system that shows others in your niche how to be successful. Then you can sell this system to people in the form of audio programs, DVDs, workbooks, and similar products.

Moving onto Ownership: If you work for others, you have no doubt thought to yourself more than once, "I could do a better job myself." If you've thought it, you owe yourself at least one shot at being entrepreneurial. You may fail at first, but the experience you gain will be invaluable. Most likely, it will embolden you to take further risks. Every rich person has a list of mistakes he or she has made. It is the way you grow.

You'll notice that these suggestions have one thing in common. They all aim to inspire, uplift, and enable others as they seek their own success within the same niche. That's the way the system is built. The more value you can offer to others, the more potential profit you can make as you lead them toward their own increased prosperity. If you don't offer people this kind of value, you are less likely to prosper yourself.

It may take time to build up to this level. I have written hundreds of articles and answered thousands of e-mails for free, slowly building my credibility and demonstrating that I actually do have something of value to offer. Then, when I charge for something like a workshop, book, or consultation, people know they are getting their money's worth.

A nurse I know started her own home-health services company. A firefighter wrote a book about home safety, then went on national television to promote it, making lots of money while helping save more lives. It's quite possible you've already been toying with similar ideas. You've watched as other people expanded within your niche. They've succeeded—so can you.

Get Rich to Support Your Niche

One of the most important lessons I hope you take away from this book is this: The way you earn money is not a reflection of your worth as a human being. You are already worthy. When you Make the Switch and realize this is true, it will become possible for you to make money in ways that are not tied directly to your niche. I am not suggesting you forsake your dreams and your deep desire to help others. My advice is not to start manufacturing widgets just for the sake of making money. It is important to keep supporting your mission somehow, or your quest for riches will feel empty.

What you need to do is make a concrete long-range plan. You need to show your mind how the money you are making will eventually support your dreams. In this way, the work you perform, no matter what it is, becomes more than just a job. It becomes a service. If you are moving toward the financial goals that will facilitate your dreams, you will be able to wake up enthused in the morning. Because your heart is involved, you'll be able to focus your mind as well. Regardless of what you find yourself doing or which job you have, you will be "on-purpose." You have probably recognized other people who are on-purpose. It may be the cashier at the local grocery store, the crossing guard at your child's school, or somebody who works in your office. You may have wondered what this person's secret was. It's not really a secret; it's a plan. People with a plan exude enthusiasm, whether they're washing cars or running corporations.

Your plan to get rich will only work if you already know your niche. You cannot work to support your dream if you have no dream. If you do have a dream and you know your niche, it is perhaps time to set off in search of the finances that will make your dream possible. This search, then, becomes part of your purpose. You work to make money to support your plan, not just to get by and pay the bills.

Of course, this kind of planning requires discipline. You need to write down specific goals and specific figures. You need actual numbers, budgets, and timelines. Your dreams need to be real dreams, not just pipe dreams.

Once you have your plan in place to support your dream, the best strategy is to totally immerse yourself in the job you need to do in order to gain financial security. That way, it's not just a job—it's an adventure. I teach the students in my massage therapy workshops that they are on a "massage adventure." You can be on an adventure within your own niche, as well.

You will need to keep refining your plan over time as the inevitable changes and challenges occur. Often, people grow into their dreams as they get older. Most philanthropists are not teenagers. It is OK for you to gradually build a life of purpose and meaning, even if that means spending months or years in the preliminary stages.

Find an Aligned Niche

Maybe your mission is not exactly right for you, and that is why you have not reached your full potential within it. When you Make the Switch, you can reassess the choices you've made earlier. You can go back and tweak your plans a little.

Often, people miss their callings by a very slight degree. Perhaps you need to align yourself a little differently to your purpose and find a parallel niche. Some people believe they are destined to be doctors, for example, when they're really meant to be in the real estate development business, specializing in hospitals and clinics. Some people feel called to teach children in the classroom, when they'd really excel as social workers who help children build better lives outside the classroom.

It is important to give yourself the mental freedom to move your mission from one aligned niche to another, to fine-tune your dreams. People can get stuck in their dream jobs, and then they turn into drudgery. Use your level of happiness and enthusiasm as a barometer. Check to see if you're stuck. Periodically realign yourself.

In today's society, it has become increasingly more common for people to hold several different positions, work for several different companies, start several different businesses, and even pursue several different careers over a lifetime. Our lives are longer, our possibilities more numerous. Why confine yourself to one self-definition?

Discover New Niches

Maybe you do not have a path or a mission. You're figuring out what it will be, or you've given up in despair after following a dream that did not pan out. Or, you're following a dream, but deep inside you know it is not the right one for you. Perhaps others have told you this is your dream, like the son whose mother tells him his dream is to become a lawyer, when he knows in his heart he wants to expand within the niche of music and performing.

It is always possible, at any age, to pursue an entirely new path. It may make sense to follow through with a career that you've already invested years in, but if following through means crushing your spirit, perhaps you should spend some time exploring other niches. Work part-time at a new job. Spend one evening a week, or one weekend a month, looking at other possibilities. Try doing something that you've always wanted to do. If this turns out not to be your niche, try something else. It is more important to follow a path with heart than to follow the so-called "right" path.

If you do eventually discover your true path, you might be able to "reverse engineer" your situation in life, turning your "real" job into the supporting role for your dream job. Perhaps your whole career was just a way to prepare you for your dream. Perhaps you have an entire second act in front of you, or even a third.

You might re-examine a niche you've pursued before but abandoned because you thought it was not for you. If you've explored certain paths to riches in the past and they did not work, try them again after you've completed the 30-day program. It is not the path that doesn't work. It is that your mind was not prepared to receive the results of following the path. Now, you may be ready.

It has been a long journey for me, but an exciting one. I never planned on getting brainwashed by a destructive cult. I did not foresee my own father kidnapping me on a Denver highway. I certainly didn't envision being imprisoned in a basement and getting deprogrammed by Ted Patrick. I didn't ask for any of this, but, looking back, I'm certainly glad it happened. The ordeal opened my mind to a whole new way of perceiving the world. Perhaps, sometimes, we need to feel what it's like to be imprisoned before we can fully appreciate freedom. Perhaps, if I hadn't been deprogrammed from a cult, I would never have even realized I also needed to be deprogrammed from the "moneyless bubble." Perhaps, like many people, I would have never even realized I was inside that bubble in the first place.

Now, I am grateful for the whole experience, even the parts that were scary or difficult. I am especially excited to be sharing the experience with you. I sincerely hope that it has given you insight that brings you closer to freeing your own mind from self-limiting beliefs.

I think the most effective way to save the Earth and uplift its people is for you and me to become Rich. The people who've dedicated their lives and livelihoods to helping others and making a difference in the world need to have more control. But we need more money to make a bigger impact. I know this is a Utopian notion; however, I also know that little things can make a big difference. If enough people Make the Switch, follow their dreams, and then contribute just a little bit more good to the world, it could make all the difference. I hope I've played a part in that process—no matter how small—through this book.

Follow your destiny. Make the Switch to living a full, Rich life. Snap out of your old programming. Destroy the myths that have held you back. You owe it to yourself and to the many others who will benefit from you becoming the strong vibrant influence you know deep inside you can be. You want to make a difference, right? You can only do that if you free yourself so you can pursue your dreams.

Freedom. True, deep freedom. This is what I wish for you.

Glossary

assault on reason: technique used by mind-control groups that involves the introduction of unreasonable or preposterous-sounding beliefs to followers, who eventually submit to these ideas and accept them as reasonable

attractions of hierarchy: the feeling that it is more pleasant and desirable to have someone "above" oneself to ascribe responsibility to, leaving one essentially blameless

catastrophe theory: French mathematician René Thom's description of those situations in which gradually changing forces lead to so-called catastrophes, or abrupt changes

cognitive science: the study of the brain's information-processing capabilities in order to understand how humans organize and make meaning of their daily bombardment of data

cult of confession: a practice used by mind-control groups that fosters self-purging of perceived shortcomings and sins

demand for purity: the practice used by mind-control groups of forcing followers to renounce outside pleasures and influences, often implemented through guilt and shame

deprogramming: to counteract or try to counteract the effect of an indoctrination, especially a cult indoctrination

dispensing of existence: the perceived power of a thought-control group to bestow purpose and meaning on a person's life

discontinuity: an out-of-time shift from one reality to another, as when an electron orbiting a nucleus is suddenly in a new orbit, with no time between the first and second states, or when a person snaps from one reality to another

doctrine over person: the practice of ascribing a higher level of importance to a credo than to the individuals who follow the credo

heavenly deception: the use of deliberate lying by cult members as long as the purpose of the lie is to further the group's seemingly righteous agenda

151

hologram: a 3-D photograph created by splitting laser beams and reassembling their interference patterns when reflected off an object

the law of experience: new information coming into a communication system (human being) tends to destroy and replace earlier information of a similar nature

karma: the belief often promoted by authoritarian groups and uncritically adhered to by millions of people that "you get what you deserve," often as a result of actions in another lifetime

loading the language: the practice of using "thought-terminating clichés" to stifle creative and individualistic thinking among thought-controlled adherents of a cult or similar group

love bombing: the deliberate use of an intense, concerted show of affection by a group of people toward an individual they seek to recruit or otherwise influence

milieu control: the monitoring of individuals' environmental influences, including books, magazines, TV, and personal interactions by other persons in control

mystical manipulation: the gradual infiltration of beliefs and thoughts into a person's mind until those beliefs seem to emanate from within the person himself

sacred science: the belief that the ideas and actions of a certain leader or group are beyond contesting or the need for proof

seduction of surrender: the sense of relief and security felt when one gives up the challenges of self-determination in exchange for easy answers supplied by an authoritarian group or individual

snapping: the sudden and complete deconstructing of an individual's belief matrix and in-group personality that has been created over time through the process of mind control

spiritual permission: the concept that, if one is following a path with a higher spiritual purpose, permission is perforce granted for any and all activities that support that purpose

synesthesia: a sensation that normally occurs in one sense modality occurs when another modality is stimulated

thought-terminating cliché: simple word or phrase used by mind-control groups to sum up complex situations, thus stifling thought

 # Resources

The Corporation by Mark Achbar, producer-director, 2005, Zeitgeist Video (documentary DVD)

Design for a Brain: The Origin of Adaptive Behavior, 2nd ed., by W. Ross Ashby, 1966, Science Paperbacks (theoretical exploration of The Law of Experience)

The Guru Papers: Masks of Authoritarian Power by Joel Kramer and Diana Alstad, 1993, North Atlantic Books

Let Our Children Go by Ted Patrick and Tom Dulack, 1979, Ballantine Books

Money is My Friend by Phil Laut, 1999, Ballantine Books

Snapping: America's Epidemic of Sudden Personality Change, 2nd ed., by Flo Conway and Jim Siegelman, 2005, Stillpoint Press

Speak and Grow Rich by Dottie Walters, 1997, Prentice Hall

Thought Control and the Psychology of Totalism: A Study of Brainwashing in China by Dr. Robert J. Lifton, 1989, University of North Carolina Press

The Trick to Money is Having Some by Stuart Wilde, 1995, Hay House

About the Author

I am an empathetic and caring person. My parents raised me that way. This led me to seek out a way to express myself and help other people, and so early in life I turned to creative writing and massage therapy. My goal? To reach out and touch the whole world through my words and healing hands. The reality? On any given day, I had to decide whether I could afford the six-inch or twelve-inch sandwich from Subway™ for lunch. The solution? I put myself through an extensive fiscal reprogramming. When I was fresh out of college, I had the life-altering experience of getting caught up in the Unification Church, or "Moonies," and subsequently getting deprogrammed by Ted Patrick, the man who invented the process. This led me to believe that I could take what I'd learned from that experience and apply it to money matters as well. When I thought about it, I realized that I'd been somehow "programmed" to feel a certain way about money. Money wasn't "spiritual" like I was, and so I shunned it. A lot of my friends and colleagues had the same problem.

My reprogramming regime consisted of haphazardly reading dozens of books and attending a plethora of wealth-building seminars, including a three-week residential retreat at a resort in Northern California. I explored encounter groups, inspirational talks, study programs, video courses, interactive DVDs, and more on my quest. It was not an overnight process, but I now find myself making $5,000 a day as a trainer, consultant, and writer, with residual royalties coming in for work I've already done. I am not a net-worth millionaire—not yet. But I am on my way. And, most importantly, on any given day I can choose exactly what it is I want to do with my time. I am my own master. My professional life is focused on helping other people achieve their vision. I am dedicated, focused, and excited about what I'm doing, which includes writing widely read books in my field like *Massage For Dummies* and *Massage Career Guide*. I have not given up on my dreams, but I have found a way to make those dreams financially viable in the real world.

It has taken me several years to change my way of thinking and increase my levels of abundance, but I have recently discovered and isolated the one key insight that finally made it possible for me to achieve wealth. This is the SWITCH that you need to make before you can truly become RICH. My hope is that this book will help you Make your own Switch to Being Rich as quickly as possible, freeing yourself from the drudgery of unwanted work, and massively expanding your positive impact in the world. Because the world needs you.

Please get in touch with comments or questions, and to discover further resources for Making the Switch at www.makingtheswitchtobeingrich.com.

more ideas. . .
more plans. . .
more resources. . .

. . .to help you reach your goals of helping exponentially more people.

Visit
www.makingtheswitchtobeingrich.com
and discover a community waiting to support you

plus

e-newsletter
mult-media programs
custom Making the Switch Journal